Fact
or
Fraud?

The Protocols of the Elders of Zion

Goran Larsson

Published by AMI-Jerusalem Center for Biblical Studies and Research
Jerusalem, San Diego, Basel, Taberg,
Nijkerk, Tokyo, Gisborne.

Fact or Fraud?
The Protocols of the Elders of Zion

For more information write to:
P.O. Box 8017, Jerusalem, Israel 91080
or
P.O. Box 22029, San Diego, California, 92192 U.S.A

Printed in Jerusalem, Israel

Photos and illustrations on pages 36, 38, 39, 40-41, and 65 are
provided by the Simon Wiesenthal Center.

Contents

Preface

The Protocols of the Elders of Zion are a perfect example of
the principle that if you tell a lie often enough, no matter how
blatant and ridiculous, it will begin to be accepted as truth. How
many times, in many different contexts and in various languages,
have the lies of *The Protocols* been repeated? Dr. Larsson points
out that only the Bible exceeds *The Protocols* in numbers printed
in this century.

There would be few Jews in the world who would not be well
aware of the evil impact of this forgery. To my amazement, I
have not found the same to be true among Christians. This is our
reason for publishing this book, *Fact or Fraud?* Today antisemitism is on the rise once again all over the world. *The Protocols*
have been one of the most effective tools of anti-Jewish forces
and has negatively affected Jewish-Christian relations. The book
also had a negative influence on Christians in many countries
who had already taken positive steps towards the Jewish people.
Christians who are not equipped with the information that *Fact
or Fraud?* provides, are at a disadvantage.

The AMI-Jerusalem Center for Biblical Studies and Research
is honored that Dr. Larsson has accepted the assignment to write
this book. His scholarship in Judaic studies and Jewish-Christian
relations eminently qualifies him to be the author. For the past
fifteen years he has served as the Director of the Swedish Theo-
logical Institute in Jerusalem. He has confronted Christian antisemitism in both its overt and covert forms in individuals from
around the world representing a broad spectrum of Christianity.

Shlomo Hizak

Jerusalem, May, 1994

Introduction

Several years ago I was astounded to hear a group of Christians seriously claiming that the then Secretary of State of the United States, Henry Kissinger, was the Antichrist. When sensing my astonishment and dismay, they tried to help me by explaining that the Antichrist will be a Jew, who will gain unlimited power, and deceive first Jews and then the whole world. Since the very effort of trying to make peace in the Middle East to them was a betrayal of the Biblical prophecies, and these efforts were engineered by Dr. Kissinger, the case was clear: the Antichrist was emerging, and he certainly was a Jew - like Christ!

I would probably have forgotten the whole incident, if not for two reasons: Even after Dr. Kissinger had retired, every now and then I heard Christians maintaining that enemy number one of the true faith - the false Messiah called Antichrist in the New Testament - would be a Jew, who would lead the whole world astray. So this was obviously a thought-pattern in certain Christian circles and not just one marginal incident. The decisive factor was, however, that I happened to study a classic antisemitic booklet, where this mindset could be detected: *The Protocols of the Elders of Zion.*

In light of the fact that this vicious publication has caused more suffering on the Jewish people in the last century than any other single document, I regard it necessary that people today should know about it - its content, history and bitter fruits.

I should make clear from the outset that I do not believe that the Christian groups mentioned above consciously had drawn their views from antisemitic sources. They were probably not antisemites but may rather considered themselves as friends of Jews and of Israel. It is equally clear though, that they had been influenced by classic antisemitic teachings without realizing it. That is what makes it particularly vicious and dangerous.

Today, in a time of resurging antisemitism, it is an imperative to recognize the features of the ugly antisemitic face. It has rightly been said that those who ignore history are doomed to repeat it. Unfortunately we cannot undo history. But we can learn from it in order to prevent its evil from being repeated. After Auschwitz every generation has a greater possibility and a deeper responsibility than ever before to study the patterns of hatred and deceit and particularly that classic evil called antisemitism.

This study aims at serving that purpose. Its scope is largely focusing on one antisemitic publication. Considering its tremendous influence up to this very day, even such a limited perspective on antisemitism is highly motivated. In his extensive book, significantly entitled *Warrant for Genocide: The Myth of the Jewish World-Conspiracy and the Protocols of the Elders of Zion*, Norman Cohn agrees with the contention "that the *Protocols of the Elders of Zion* was probably the most widely distributed book in the world after the Bible, and certainly the myth of the Jewish world-conspiracy was a potent factor in the shaping of world history." But he continues, "Today the whole story is already almost forgotten - so much so that it is quite rare, at least in Europe, to meet anyone under the age of forty who has even heard of those strange ideas."[1]

Unfortunately, this statement a quarter of a century ago is no longer accurate. Even if the source to a large extent may have been forgotten, the ideas continue to flourish and bear their bitter fruits. *The Protocols of the Elders of Zion* have rightly been called the Bible of antisemitism, not only used by Hitler, Stalin and other enemies of mankind in the past. Still a bestseller, they continue their poisoning of the minds of new generations all over the world. Therefore, it is necessary to unearth their roots again and again, display the fruits and - hopefully - finally be able to cast out this evil to the place where it forever belongs: On the trash heap of human history.

---

1   p.17. This is still the best scholarly book on *The Protocols*, containing an extensive bibliography on various editions of the *Protocols* and secondary literature. The first scholarly presentation of the origins of the forgery in English was made by Herman Bernstein in 1935. Here we find the full text of *The Protocols* together with the other texts on which they are based (in English translation). A thorough German investigation was published ten years earlier by B.Segel. For these and other references, see bibliography.

I.
The Roots of a Lie

1. THE LIE

The Protocols of the Elders of Zion claim to be the minutes of an alleged conference for the senior leaders of world Jewry, named the "Elders of Zion." The document is divided into 24 chapters, in which a satanic Jewish plot to conquer and enslave the whole world is spelled out. A brief summary of this imaginary conspiracy may be sufficient to demonstrate the monstrosity ascribed to the Jews:

The Protocols describe Jews as a group of secret, subversive infiltrators who do not shun from any means of securing world dominion. They spread diseases, instigate disorder, revolutions and wars in order to overthrow the rulers of the nations and undermine the society. A main target is also Christianity, and a main method is to give freedom and rights to the people, who can then be easily manipulated by Jews and stirred up against the existing political and religious authorities. One compliant - it is stated - is the secret international order of the Freemasons, which is said to be the invisible machinery in the hands of Jews. Together they have already masterminded the French revolution in 1789 and launched its concept of "liberty, equality, fraternity" (see also p.25).

Since then, according to *The Protocols*, they have worked for the emancipation of the masses by giving them freedom of speech and freedom of religion. The right to vote and the creation of parliamentary democracies are presented as part of the same plan. Political and religious liberty among the masses will namely cause the loss of authority of both the existing aristocratic leadership and of the church:

"In the days when the people looked on their sovereigns as on the will of God, they quietly submitted to the despotism of their monarchs. But from the day that we inspired the populace with the idea of its own rights, they began to regard kings as ordinary mortals. In the eye of the mob the holy ointment fell from the head of the monarchs, and, when we took away their religion, the power was thrown into the streets like public property, and was snatched up by us" (5th protocol).

In the light of this antimonarchic and anti-Christian view of the alleged "Elders of Zion," they are not only behind liberalism but also socialism and communism. With the press as their instrument and the banks as their power and with all the necessary international contacts in their hand, Jews are now close to their goal, that is, the creation of a world government under their leadership. They will just have to instigate chaos and anarchy among the nations in order to dissolve them from within. Therefore they provoke war between the classes by various means, e.g. by stirring up the workers against the employers, inflicting strikes and causing starvation by increasing prices:

"Our strength lies in keeping the working man in perpetual want and impotence; because, by so doing, we retain him subject to our will..."

(3rd protocol)

They take control over education in order to foster ignorance and cause moral disintegration. For the case that all this should fail, they finally have a sinister plan prepared:

"Metropolitan railways and underground passages will be constructed in all cities. From these subterranean places we will explode all the cities of the world, together with their institutions and documents" (9th protocol).

And alas, as if this were not enough, Jews will also be able to stir up wars between the nations. Having dissolved the existing order, they will have reached their goal. For then the nations of the world will be so exhausted by the tribulations inflicted upon them by Jews, that they will accept anyone who may save them. Once in power, they will then demand blind obedience to their Jewish king:

> "When the populace noticed that it was being given all sorts of rights in the name of liberty, it imagined itself to be the master, and tried to assume power. Of course, like every other blind man, the mass came up against innumerable obstacles. Then, as it did not wish to return to the former regime, it lays its power at our feet... We have led the nations from one disappointment to another, so that they should even renounce us in favor of the King-Despot of the blood of Zion, whom we are preparing for the world" (3rd protocol).

Now the great moment has come when they will be able to establish the world government, led by "the World Ruler, sprung from the Holy seed of David..."[2]

2. ITS ROOTS

The deepest roots of these fantasies can be traced back to the conception of the Jews as demons, which was a consequence of the rivalry between early Christianity and Judaism. In the first Christian centuries there was not only an ongoing controversy between them regarding the belief in Jesus of Nazareth, but also a struggle for converts among the pagans, who were gradually losing their faith in the Greek and Roman gods. Both Judaism and Christianity preached *one* God, and both were attractive alternatives to the old idolatry. As we can learn from the letters of Paul, the Christian faith spread rapidly among the Gentiles all over the Mediterranean area, and so did Judaism. The synagogues were thronged with Gentiles, called "God-fearers," who had started to believe in the one, true God, the God of Israel.

There is no doubt that in many areas and in certain times Judaism was even more successful among the Gentiles than Christianity. In such a situation of antagonism, it was certainly a

---

2   The quotations are taken from the extracts in Cohn p.275-288. For the full text, see Bernstein p.295-359.

temptation for Christians to present Jews as the arch-enemies of Christ and even apply certain passages in the New Testament regarding the "Antichrist" to them - such as Matthew 24,24; 2 Thessalonians 2,1ff; 1 John 2,18ff; 4,3; Revelation 13. In this bitter spirit the early fathers of the Church, such as Tertullian (160-225 A.D.), Augustine and John Chrysostom (both born in 354 A.D.), produced the infamous *Adversus Judaeos*-literature, that is, writings "against the Jews." Here the synagogues were described as dwelling-places of demons and devils and Jews as cursed by God, sons of Satan and empowered with black magic and all sorts of evil.

A second reason for the growing hatred against Jews was certainly also the fact that many Christians within the church itself were following Jewish practices. Such "judaizers" were regarded as heretics, who had not understood the total break between the old and the new order. In order to fight them, Judaism as such - and occasionally even the Old Testament - was presented as inferior, anti-Christian and hostile to God and man.[3]

The Jew as a symbol of hatred; pre-war Rumania.

When Christianity, having been a persecuted minority itself, became an empowered state religion in the 4th century, this hatred became a tragedy. Judaism was banned as a heresy, and antisemitism was exported even into areas where there were no, or hardly any, Jews present (see p.37,54,72). As representatives of the Old Testament and as the opponents of the gospel of Christ, they became a stereotyped symbol of evil. They allegedly intended to thwart God's plans and

---

3   See further the bibliography, particularly the works of Davies, Flannery, Gager, Hay Klein, Littell, Nicholls and Parkes. Nicholls' excellent book is the most recent study.

were seen as the dangerous enemies of all mankind and in particular of the church.

In this realm of thought it is not surprising that centuries later they were accused of the most horrendous crimes. When epidemics raged, for instance the Black Death in the 14th century, they were accused of poisoning the wells as one method of ruining and conquering the Christians. A common accusation was the "blood-

The blood-libel accusation; Germany 15th century.

libel", that is, ritual slaughter of Christian children in order to use their blood for the unleavened Passover bread. They were charged of desecrating the holy communion bread by piercing it and trampling on it. Behind these two accusations lies the ancient myth of the Jews as having killed Christ - and even God himself (*deicide*)[4] - and whose hatred of Christ and God continued throughout the ages, forcing them to try to repeat their evil deeds.

In the light of such an approach, every evil that emerged could be "explained" through Jewish intrigues and vile of demonic dimensions. They became the scapegoat that so often is sought for in times of distress. The fact that the Jewish communities often were forced into ghettos and thus led a life which was not immediately open to the surrounding society, made the myths of their secret conspiracies even more credible in the eyes of the public.[5]

This general sketch of the deepest roots of *The Protocols*, however important it may be, is not sufficient to explain the detailed plot described there. These were published for the first time in the beginning of our century, that is, in an era when one had hoped that such superstitions should have vanished, just as the myths surrounding the witch-hunts three-hundred years earlier. It seems, however, that when the ancient traditions which victimized the Jews in the name of Christianity became outdated, they were modernized in two ways: First of all, the idea of a Jewish conspiracy to combat God and his church on earth, the basis of which was primarily *religious*, was translated into *political* and *racist* terms. If in previous times the main target had been their allegedly inferior and false *religion*, now they were primarily depicted as a subversive *social group* or an inferior *race*. Secondly, this idea was tailored to fit into the historical events on the political scene in Europe during the 19th and the beginning of the 20th century.[6]

In this way the soil was prepared for antisemitism even among secular people who did not care for religion and "Christian" explanations. Such a popularization obviously gave the earlier supersti-

---

4   Thus already Melito of Sardis contends in his Easter Sermon: "He who hung the earth is hanging; he who fixed the heavens has been fixed; he who fastened the universe has been fastened to a tree; the Sovereign has been insulted; the God has been murdered; the King of Israel has been put to death by an Israelite right hand" (*Peri Pascha*, lines 711-716; quoted by Nicholls p.177f).

5   An excellent survey of the medieval anti-Jewish myths is given by Nicholls in the chapter "Popular Paranoia", p.225-259. See also Trachtenberg's extensive book specializing on this subject.

6   Cohn p.16 is to the point when contending that *The Protocols* are "a modernized, secularized version of the popular medieval view of Jews as a league of sorcerers employed by Satan for the spiritual and physical ruination of Christendom." See further the chapter about "Secular Antisemitism" in Nicholls p.313-349.

tious conceptions of Jews the potential to revive, when certain circumstances in society provided the favorable conditions for growth (see p.27ff,51).

There are several important milestones in the revival process of this ancient myth of hatred. I will limit myself to four publications, beginning with the final product - *The Protocols* themselves.

1. *The Protocols of the Elders of Zion*

The first edition appeared in Russia in 1905.[7] It was then only incorporated as an appendix in a larger book from 1901, the title of which clearly reveals its purpose and content: *The Great in the Little: Antichrist Considered as an Imminent Political Possibility.* It was written by a Russian Orthodox Christian, Sergei Nilus, who was fully convinced that the Antichrist was emerging in his own days, and that the end of the world was at hand. Since the Antichrist would be the Messiah of the Jews, they would play a decisive role in the last turbulent events of this era. Consequently, he must have regarded it as a marvelous confirmation of these ideas, when he came across *The Protocols* and was able to add them to the third edition of his book four years later. In his commentary to *The Protocols* he writes among others:

> "There is no room left for doubt. With all the might and terror of Satan, the reign of the triumphant King of Israel is approaching our unregenerate world; the King born of the blood of Zion - the Antichrist - is near to the throne of universal power."[8]

In 1911 he edited *The Protocols* as a separate book for the first time. Nine years later German and English translations were published, which since then have been translated to most of the larger modern languages in the world (see p.40f).

The Protocols are anonymous; the subject is a vague "we." Neither are they related to a particular place nor to a specific date.

---

7   An abbreviated version had actually appeared already in 1903 in the newspaper *Znamia* (The Banner).
8   Quoted from Cohn p.288.

Сергѣй Нилусъ.

Великое

въ маломъ

и

АНТИХРИСТЪ,

какъ близкая политическая возможность.

ЗАПИСКИ ПРАВОСЛАВНАГО.

(ИЗДАНІЕ ВТОРОЕ, ИСПРАВЛЕННОЕ И ДОПОЛНЕННОЕ).

ЦАРСКОЕ СЕЛО.
Типографія Царскосельскаго Комитета Краснаго Креста.
1905.

The first edition of *The Protocols of the Elders of Zion*.

These circumstances led immediately to speculations regarding their authenticity. When tracing their origins, it is illuminating to take a look at their first editor. Sergei Nilus was active at the turn of the century, when apocalyptic and eschatological expectations were widespread in religious circles. Moreover, in those days the authoritarian government of the Tsar was heavily pressed by strikes and fervent demands among the people for democracy and freedom. In 1905 it finally had to concede to social reforms and a liberal constitution.

Nilus was a devoted nationalist and supporter of the Tsar. In this situation he presumed to be almost a prophetic savior of ancient Russia against the dangers of the new age, claiming that these were in reality the result of a huge attack from satanic, anti-Christian powers. He could find strong support from the feared reactionary secret police, to whom he was linked as a clerical official. Other frustrated conservative and antidemocratic forces were prone to embrace such ideas, the most notorious being a party called "The Union of the Russian People" or "The Black Hundreds." They instigated numerous pogroms all over Russia in which thousands of Jews, as well as other people regarded as liberals and radicals, were brutally murdered (see p.31). Needless to say, even the Russian Orthodox Church provided a good market for Nilus' ideas. It may be enough to exemplify the link between the antisemitic, nationalistic forces and the church by the fact that Nilus' edition of *The Protocols* was immediately ordered to be read in all the churches of Moscow!

The question of their origin, however, soon became critical. Nilus himself was blindfolded by his antisemitism and eschatological expectations and probably believed them to be genuine. First he claimed to have received them from a person who said he had stolen them from Zionist archives in Paris. Later he ascribed them to the first Zionist congress in Basel 1897. This certainly did not serve his case, since that congress had been held in the open with all the minutes published. Other desperate efforts to uphold their genuineness could not withstand a serious examination either. It did not help that Nilus had published them in order to defend the tsarist regime; their falsity was obvious to any serious analyst. Eventually the Tsar himself reluctantly labeled them as antisemitic propaganda and had them confiscated after having been convinced that they were spurious: "Drop *The Protocols*. One cannot defend a pure cause by dirty methods."[9] Such a concession, even from the one whose interest they served, was certainly a setback to the antisemitic propagandists.

Even Nilus himself seems to have had doubts. When asked whether he might not be working with a forgery, he is said to have answered:

> "You know my favorite quotation from St. Paul? - 'The power of God works through human weakness.' Let us admit that *the Protocols* are spurious. But can't God use them to unmask the iniquity that is being prepared? Didn't Balaam's ass prophesy? Can't God, for the sake of our faith, change dog's bones into miracle-working relics? So he can put the announcement of truth into a lying mouth."[10]

This is the true face of the kind of blindfolded religious fanaticism that throughout the ages has blasphemed God's name and been instrumental in so much human suffering!

Thus the spuriousness of *The Protocols* was more or less admitted even in antisemitic circles. It would take till 1921, however, till the origins of the forgery were found and conclusive proofs against their authenticity could finally be provided.

2. *Dialogue in Hell between Montesquieu and Machiavelli* (*Dialogue aux Enfers entre Montesquieu et Machiavel*)

The one who eventually found the main source of *The Protocols* was an English correspondent of "The Times" in Constantinople, Philip Graves. A Russian who had fled to Turkey after the revolution in 1917 showed him a book in French, which he had bought from an officer of the former tsarist secret police. After

---

9   Cohn p.115.
10   The quote is taken from an article published in 1921 by a person who knew Nilus very closely. This article, the full text of which appears in Bernstein p.360-369, gives a vivid impression of the weird state of mind that characterized Nilus. See also the chapter called "A Visit to Nilus" in Curtiss p.61-72.

some research it became clear that the book, first published in Belgium in 1864, was a political satire written by a French lawyer, Maurice Joly. It consists of 25 fictitious dialogues in the underworld between one politician - the Italian Machiavelli (1469-1527) - and one political philosopher - the Frenchman Montesquieu (1689-1755).[11] Through his politics, the notorious Machiavelli has become almost the embodiment of an unscrupulous politician; in Webster's dictionary the term "Machiavellianism" is defined as "The doctrine of Machiavelli that denies the relevance of morality in political affairs." Contrary to this, Montesquieu is known as an advocate of freedom of thought and of humanitarian and democratic values.

The purpose of this antagonistic dialogue was to attack the French Emperor Napoleon III (1808-1873), whose reactionary politics Maurice Joly passionately detested. In order to do so, he made Machiavelli the camouflaged mouthpiece of the emperor, revealing the true purpose of his cruel and cynical methods. By writing a work of fiction, Joly hoped to escape French censorship. His edition was, however, confiscated at the French border. This probably explains why his book was so little known that it took till 1921 until someone discovered that this was the prime source of *The Protocols*.

When reading the book, Philip Graves immediately realized what the Russian pointed out to him: Large parts of the dialogue had been copied almost literally into *The Protocols* - altogether about 60%. Even the order and structure of *The Protocols* with their 24 chapters follow the 25 dialogues in Joly's book.[12] A comparison between a passage in the twelfth dialogue and in the twelfth "protocol" may suffice to illustrate the obvious forgery. Machiavelli states:

> "Like the god Vishnu, my press will have a hundred arms, and these arms will give expression to all shades of opinion throughout the whole country. People will belong to my party without realizing it. Those who think they are talking their own language

11   For the full text, see Bernstein p.75-258.
12   An interesting article from 1921, in which Graves describes his discovery of the plagiarism, is found in Bernstein p.259-264.

will be talking mine, those who think they are stirring up people on their side will be stirring up people on mine, those who think they are marching under their flag will be marching under mine."

The claim of the "Elders" is almost identical:

"These newspapers, like the Indian god Vishnu, will be possessed of hundreds of hands, each of which will be feeling the pulse of varying public opinion... If any chatterers are going to imagine that they are repeating the opinion of their party newspaper, they will in reality be repeating our own opinion, or the opinion which we desire. Thinking that they are following the organ of this party, they will in reality be following the flag which we will fly for them."[13]

The Protocols were unequivocally revealed as a blatant plagiarism, with one simple but ill-fated difference: the despotic politics of Napoleon III, voiced by Machiavelli, to suppress the people in France, were now ascribed to the Jews in conspiracy against the whole world!

Later, antisemites tried to uphold the authenticity of *The Protocols* by claiming that Maurice Joly actually was a Jew, who indirectly revealed a Jewish plan. They were, however, never able to substantiate their desperate claim. The contrary is true. It was proved that Joly was a Christian. Further, the very fact that Jews appear only once in his book - and then in a disparaging way - makes the claim not only improbable but ridiculous.

The forger was most probably a Russian antisemitic nationalist and supporter of the Tsar against the revolutionary forces. Consequently, he opposed the values of freedom and democracy, which Joly supported. When plagiarizing Joly's book, the not very smart forger therefore ended up with bizarre inconsistencies and contradictions. He had to attribute to Jews not only Machiavelli's

---

13 In Bernstein p. 371-397, Cohn p.275-279, and Curtiss p.95-106, excerpts from the two documents are quoted in parallel versions to facilitate the comparison.

but also Montesquieu's ideas, however irreconcilable they were! As a result *The Protocols* could be used by antisemites in the most disparate context to ascribe virtually any opinion that they disliked to Jews: liberalism and communism, capitalism and socialism etc. They could be applied to almost any situation in order to "prove" Jewish involvement. This is what actually happened, when the bitter fruits of this forgery later ripened (see p.36,50f,64).

In 1921 Graves published his evidence in *The Times*. The year before this newspaper had carried a review of *The Protocols*, in which it was hinted that the Jews might actually stand behind England's archenemy, Germany. The immediate effect of Graves' article was that the further publication of *The Protocols* in England was limited to minor fanatic antisemitic groups. Eventually his article also hampered their influence worldwide.

It also came to play a decisive role in the famous Bern trial in 1934-35. The Jewish communities in Switzerland sued those who stood behind the distribution of *The Protocols* - mostly Nazis who were affiliated with Germany. The trial led to a much publicized investigation of the sources of *The Protocols* with a conclusive verdict. Confirming their spuriousness, the court in its verdict used expressions such as "ridiculous nonsense," "defamation" and "inflammatory writings."[14]

One main branch is still missing in the twisted root system of *The Protocols*. For not even the remolding of Joly's dialogue into a meeting of Jewish leaders originated from the forger. He actually adapted that idea from another literary composition:

3. *The Rabbi's Speech*

Joly's book was written to promote the liberating political forces but was abused by antisemites for their purposes. The author of the next work, however, was an antisemite himself. His name was Hermann Goedsche, who wrote for a German (Prussian) nationalistic and conservative newspaper. Under the pseudonym of Sir John Ratcliffe he published a novel in 1868, called

14   A summary of the trial is given by Cohn p.220-231 and Curtiss p.73-93.

Biarritz, which contained a chapter with the ominous title "In the Jewish Cemetery in Prague."

What happens there is an imagined convocation at midnight between the spirits of representatives of the twelve tribes of Israel, presided over by a levitical descendant from the high priest Aaron. They meet once every century to report on their past activities in the world. In these reports we find most of the ingredients of the classic antisemitic stereotypes: Robbing land from the Christians through treachery, destroying churches, corrupting morale, obtaining gold, empowering the working class, instigating upheavals and unrest and gaining political power, controlling the market and the media and at the end enslaving the whole world under their god - the golden calf! This ultimate goal is to be reached, by the time they meet after another hundred years.

Even though being part of a fictitious novel, it can no doubt be characterized as "the basis for a very influential antisemitic forgery,"[15] that is, for *The Protocols*. Similar to Russia thirty years later, in those days a strong democratic movement in Germany claimed full civil rights for all inhabitants, including the Jews. This was actually realized three years after the publication of Goedsche's novel. No wonder then, that it came to be used by reactionary forces which opposed the emancipation of Jews in countries where similar forces were working. As so often throughout history, Jews became the hate object of people who opposed certain developments in their days: the rise of commerce and industry, the emergence of a free press, the decline of religion, the emancipation of the lower classes etc.

Soon such frustrated people had this particular chapter of Goedsche's novel published separately as an authentic record of a real meeting between Jewish leaders. Eventually the most common version claimed that a certain chief rabbi had given a speech to leading Jews at a secret meeting; then the pamphlet became known as *The Rabbi's Speech*.[16] The first separate publication appeared in Russia in 1872. It was widely distributed and came later

15   Cohn p.34.
16   For the full text, see Bernstein p.285-292 and Cohn p.269-274.

to play a gloomy role in warranting the subsequent numerous pogroms in Russia.

The contradictions between the various publications regarding the identity of the rabbi and the Jewish leaders, and the place for the meeting, did not prevent the pamphlet from being disseminated as authentic - just as *The Protocols* - all over Europe for more than half a century. Very often *The Rabbi's Speech* and *The Protocols* were published together and used to mutually prove their genuineness.

The very idea of a secret, central Jewish meeting aiming at world control, was taken over from *The Rabbi's Speech* by the Russian forger of *The Protocols*. This discovery was actually presented by Herman Bernstein (see the bibliography) already some months before Philip Graves discovered the link between *The Protocols* and *The Dialogue* in a book called *The History of a Lie*, which was published in early 1921.

The forger of *The Protocols* may also have used other similar antisemitic fabrications, which circulated particularly in times of political instability and in times when the social situation of Jews was improving.

4. *The Simonini Letter*

Thus an even older version of the myth of a universal Jewish plot behind the tribulations of history is found in a widely spread document, called *The Simonini Letter*, from 1806. It is a letter supposedly written by an Italian army officer, called J.B.Simonini. Nothing is known about him, but he claims to have pretended to be a Jew as a way of getting access to the age-old sinister plans of Jews, which he could now present. Already this bogus report contains the basic elements of later antisemitic writings: the hatred of Jews for the Church, their machinations to infiltrate everywhere in order to enslave Christians and become the world rulers etc.

The setting in which it emerged was France in the time of Napoleon (1769-1821). Just like in Germany in 1868 and in Russia at the turn of the century, this was a time of social reforms in France. Napoleon struggled to grant civil rights even to Jews. The French Jews were actually the first ones in Europe to be emancipated. The same pattern as we have seen before repeats itself even here.

A symbolic representation of Christianity and Judaism - the latter blindfolded with a broken staff; the cathedral in Strasbourg, 13th century. Triumphalistic images such as these entail the deepest roots of antisemitism.

In reactionary groups which acted against Napoleon's policy, this fake letter was conceived in order to appoint a scapegoat.

Till those days the time had not been ripe to accuse Jews of causing the French revolution; too many knew the fact that no Jews had played any role in the revolution. Instead the Freemasons had been the scapegoat. The *Simonini Letter* paved the way for a thought that gradually became very common in antisemitic circles, namely that there was an alliance between Jews and the Freemasons, and that Jews nevertheless stood behind the French revolution![17] *The Protocols* adapted much of the ancient antimasonic ideas and ascribed them both to Jews and to an imagined Jewish-Masonic conspiracy. Sometimes even a German Bavarian society called "Illuminati" was an alleged partner of the plot. The fact that this group was partly anti-Jewish and ceased to exist already in 1786, and that the Freemasons in certain areas and periods of time did not even accept Jews as members at all, did not bother the adherents of these allegations. They were later to be taken up by both Hitler and Stalin and by conspiratory theorists up to the present time.

To sum up: A large part of the content of *The Protocols* was directly plagiarized from Joly's book, supplemented by *The Rabbi's Speech* and maybe other similar fabrications, which also provided the forger with the contextual frame of the content.

17   See William Korey, "The Freemason-Zionist Plot," in: *Midstream* 32,6, June-July, 1986, p.15-20.

II.
The Fruits of a Lie

1. PREPARING THE GROUND

Even though there was unanimous proof that *The Protocols* were a fake already in 1921, this did not stop their continuous dissemination. On the contrary, it was only now, after the First World War and the Russian revolution, that they got an outreach and an acceptance in circles far outside minor fanatical groups. Only in 1920 English, American, German, French and Polish editions were published, and new versions appeared in large editions almost every year thereafter.

This cannot only be explained through the general human readiness of believing fantastic and exciting "disclosures." The more direct explanation can - again - be found in the turbulent conditions which prevailed in Europe after a bloody world war and a Communist revolution which were changing the social and political map of the world. In Germany a scapegoat was looked for as an explanation of the war failure and the subsequent unemployment and economical collapse. In Russia monarchists and counter-revolutionaries were in a state of shock after their defeat. In both cases the ground was fertile for a seed that since long had been sown by antisemitic groups, yet with relatively limited success so far.

The fast growth of the antisemitic myth of a Jewish world conspiracy as described in *The Protocols* was nevertheless not limited to Germany and Russia. All over Europe the fear of communism, socialism and revolution was widespread. German and exiled Russian antisemites were aggressive in establishing contacts in other countries, where poverty and political insurgency prevailed as well. The antisemitic export was thriving. Incredible though it sounds, in the years between the two world wars *The Protocols* were translated into virtually all European languages. New editions were constantly printed. They also reached South

Africa, the U.S., Canada and Latin America. Even China and Japan received their dose of this antisemitic poison!

In the U.S. they received a surprising support from the automotive industrialist Henry Ford. He was convinced by a Russian monarchist to have *The Protocols* published and commented on, first in his newspaper *The Dearborn Independent*, then in a separate book, which was translated into 16 languages and distributed by the millions: *The International Jew. The World's Foremost Problem. Being a Reprint of a Series of Articles Appearing in The Dearborn Independent from May 22 to October 2, 1920* (see p.31f). The headings of a few chapters are sufficient to give an impression of the spirit behind this publication: I. The Jew in Character and Business... VI. Jewish Question Breaks Into the Magazines... VIII. Does a Definite Jewish World Program Exist? ... X. An Introduction to the "Jewish Protocols"... XII. "Jewish Protocols" Claim Part Fulfillment... XIV. Did the Jews Foresee the World War? ... XIX. The All-Jewish Mark on "Red Russia." XX. Jewish Testimony in Favor of Bolshevism.[18]

It is obvious that this explication of *The Protocols* capitalized on the "Red Scare" and the abhorrence of the persecution of Christians by the Communists; that religious Jews were just as much persecuted was an unknown or ignored fact. Thus, there was a market for the idea of an invisible Jewish world-government behind communism and socialism as well as the current notions of tolerance and liberalism, modern fashion, music and film industry. Almost everything that was regarded as undermining religious moral and faith could be labeled as "Jewish." To support the bizarre defamation it was often enough to point at one single Jew as being involved in the feared activities or as contenders of the ideas criticized. These Jews were allegedly agents of world Jewry, serving the ultimate evil (cf. p.53,71). Thus we read in the chapter called "Jewish Plan to Split Society by Ideas" (p.151) the following reference to *The Protocols*:

---

18 On this and other antisemitic publications in the U.S. after the First World War, see Robert Singerman, "The American Career of the *Protocols of the Elders of Zion*," in: *American Jewish History* 71, 1981, p.48-78. For more extensive studies, see Robert Lacey, *Ford, the Men and the Machine*, Little, Brown, Boston, 1986, particularly p.205-219; Albert Lee, *Henry Ford and the Jews*, Stein and Day, New York, 1980.

"We will so wear out and exhaust the Gentiles by all this, that they will be compelled to offer us an international authority, which by its position will enable us to absorb without disturbance all the governmental forces of the world and thus form a super-government."

One of the most common ways of advocating the truth behind the lies of *The Protocols* was to claim that the actual chaotic events of this century proved them to be true: Had there not indeed been anarchy, revolutions, wars and a financial collapse, just as described in *The Protocols*? Strangely enough it was concluded that also the rest had to be true, namely that Jews were behind these tribulations. Needless to say, this is *circular reasoning*. The axiomatic starting point is that Jews cause all the evil. Evil things actually take place. Therefore Jews must cause all this evil!

Such paranoiac fear of Jews as a potential subversive world power characterized the publication of *The Protocols* even in other countries. The editions were often extensively prefaced and commented on in order to popularize them and apply them to contemporary problems. In England they were 'updated' to describe either a Jewish-Communist or a Jewish-German conspiracy against England - or both! In the strong Catholic country of Poland the link between the Jews and the anti-Christian Bolsheviks was the main motif; the fact that most Jews there were religious and bitter opponents of communism did not help.

The same religious antisemitism also played an important role in France, where the influence of *The Protocols* between the world wars was tremendous; more than 30 editions appeared together with elaborate commentaries. They fueled the Fascists in Italy. In Spain they were widely quoted by the propagandists, in order to prepare the people for General Franco's antisemitic New Year's speech in 1939. On the other side of the political specter they boosted the paranoia of Stalin, when he turned against Jews (see p.36). In addition to the direct influence by *The Protocols*, maybe the largest outreach and impact was still given through a countless number of popular pamphlets and articles in newspapers worldwide, which were built on their content.

Thus, the most distributed and believed falsification of all time was already an established fact, when the political climate transformed this evil seed into a harvest of death. The ground was prepared. The fruits were ripe.

2. THE FRUITS

Sometimes people say that the important thing is not so much what we think but what we do. After having witnessed the evil fruits of the antisemitic lie, we ought to be careful of what thoughts are planted in people's minds. One day they may form the patterns of their actions. The worst genocide in human history began with the planting of suspicion and hatred and with the poisoning of thoughts.

We have seen that the roots of antisemitic lies are deep. Without those deep roots and the soil widely prepared through a persistent defamation of the Jews, there would hardly have been such bitter fruits as witnessed during the German Nazi regime. As long as anti-Judaism was only religiously motivated, there was - with few exceptions like the Crusades - a limit as to how far the hatred could be put into practice. That barrier was set by the biblical commandment against murder. Martin Luther and others advocated the expulsion of Jews, the burning the synagogues and talmudic writings and most of the atrocities committed by the Nazis (see p.56f). But they certainly did not give a warrant for genocide.

Secular antisemitism, however, did not necessarily adhere to this last moral barrier. The religious teaching of contempt throughout the previous centuries nevertheless was a decisive factor, which made the final step possible. This applies not only to the genocide directly committed by the Nazis but also to the easiness with which they could get their obedient and willing collaborators. And above all, it is the main explanation of the unbelievable indifference that characterized the populations of the occupied countries and the world at large as passive bystanders.

This may sound unfair in the light of the heroic struggle of the Allies. I am, however, referring precisely to the fact that the Jewish sufferings were met with passivity by most nations and churches who otherwise abhorred the Nazis.[19] Jews were caught in a death trap, when one country after another closed their doors to the doomed Jewish nation, vilified and accused of crime towards mankind by those who committed such a crime themselves. Antisemitism had obviously infected the minds to such an extent that it had paralyzed the whole body of world society and made it unable to resist and react! This certainly is a fruit of antisemitism, almost as dangerous and tragic as the genocide itself. It was this evil fruit that made the final harvest possible.

There had been, however, frightening precedents in the decades before the outbreak of the Second World War. In Russia the antisemites had already reaped the fruits of the imaginations in publications like *The Rabbi's Speech* and *The Protocols*. Over and over again it is obvious that the pogroms, which resulted in more than 100,000 Jews massacred in the first two decades of this century, were preceded by massive antisemitic propaganda. The false accusations of Jews of all sorts of evil were used to cover the pogroms, and the pogroms to divert the attention of the people from the real causes behind the social misery. This was actually an ominous prelude to the Holocaust, which ought to have alarmed the world. Today it is largely forgotten, overshadowed as it is by the Nazi genocide.

The pattern is, however, the same. The Nazis understood and exploited the connection between thought and deed. Before they put their demonic plans into action, they worked hard to influence the thinking of the people. *The Protocols* became the major staple of the antisemitic propaganda. Together with *The Rabbi's Speech* they were for instance made an obligatory part of the curriculum at schools already in 1935. The obsession and fervor with which they pursued their antisemitic goals was of course unmoved by Herman Bernstein's and Philip Graves' publications of the spurious origins of *The Protocols* and by the subsequent Bern trial. Less dogmatic antisemites were eventually convinced by such conclusive evidence; in 1927 Henry Ford issued a public apology, closed down his newspaper and stopped further publication of *The International Jew*. He could, however, not stop the German Nazis

---

19   See the important study of Martin Gilbert, *Auschwitz and the Allies,* Holt, Rinehart, and Winston, New York, 1982.

from using his book and promoting it worldwide together with the whole pack of lies that could possibly serve their purpose.

As we have seen, Sergei Nilus, the first editor of *The Protocols*, was not even concerned with their truth, hoping that they, in any case, would support his preconceived ideas. Similarly Hitler's minister of propaganda, Joseph Goebbels, cynically contended that if a lie was repeated often enough, the people would finally believe it. In the first case we see a paranoiac fanatic, who detects a conspiracy behind everything that contradicts his world-view. In the second case we face a callous architect of mass murder, who uses the lie to create an attitude among the people that enables him to realize his murderous plans.

There are as a matter of fact few people of Goebbels' caliber, but there are more people like Nilus. And even more who are apt to fall victim to a simplified world-view, according to which there has to be a hidden hand behind the awkward things that cannot be fully understood. Particularly in times of upheavals and distress many people do not even seriously ask the simple question about the truth. They are the ones who first fall prey to Goebbels' strategy regarding the repeated lie: There must be some truth to it...

The evil fruits of the antisemitic myths of a half century ago are well-known. However, even before the Holocaust, *The Protocols* could rightly be characterized in this way: "It is no exaggeration to say that they cost the lives of many thousands of innocent persons and that more blood cling to their pages than to those of any other mendacious document in the world's history."[20] Today this condemning judgment is more true than ever.

---

20   Valentin p.165. All of chapter IX, p.165-183, deals with *The Protocols*.

III.
The Survival of a Lie

With Auschwitz and the "final solution" behind, it is unbelievable that this black chapter of human inhumanity is not concluded. But it is not just a paragraph in the history books. Tragically enough we are dealing with an evil that has not only left frightful traces behind but is still on the move. Unfortunately this booklet is not only of historical interest. Actually, *The Protocols* are so absurd and senseless, that they would not deserve any attention at all, had it not been for their continuous pernicious influence in wide circles up to this very day. As a matter of fact vitriolic antisemitism seems to exert more influence and gain more ground in recent years than ever since the destruction of European Jewry during the Second World War. Antisemitism certainly did not die with Hitler.

Someone has said: The only thing we can learn from history is that man does not learn from history. The survival - and constant revival - of *The Protocols* gives clear and distinct evidence of these words. Therefore, our dealing with them ninety years after their first appearance, needs no justification. To be ignorant of their deep roots, bitter fruits and continued growth would be highly irresponsible and dangerous.

The ugly face of antisemitism has many different features. Yet, it is basically the same. In order to recognize it, whenever, wherever and however it appears, we need to be familiar with these features. The survival of *The Protocols* after the Holocaust reveals more traits of this age-old phenomenon of human evil - sometimes disguised even under other names and promoted by influential and respectable people. A survey of its influence in the postwar era will substantiate this.

Such a survey shows that primarily four main circles provided the soil for the survival and resurgence of the antisemitic lie:

1) The communist and socialist world under the leadership of the former Soviet Union. 2) Islam and the Arab world. 3) Ultra-nationalists and neo-Nazis. 4) Certain groups of conservative, liberal and left-wing Christians.

The lowest common denominator for these highly disparate and antagonistic groups, who otherwise have virtually nothing in common, is the discrimination and hatred of Jews. This is, however, not surprising. We have learnt that *The Protocols* ascribe the most contradictory views to Jews. Consequently, every adherent of each one of these mutually exclusive opinions, could regard the Jews as the representatives of their opponents. We will also see that all the various facets of classic and modern antisemitism - religious, political and racial - survived.

We begin with the country where *The Protocols* have their deepest roots:

1. The Former Soviet Union and the Communist World

Even in postwar history the Russians are forerunners in disseminating *The Protocols* and their ideas. When they were first published in Russia, they were the product of frustrated and paranoiac defenders of a crumbling tsarist empire. After their defeat during the Russian revolution, *The Protocols* lost their significance in Russia, at least for a time. Instead, the Germans took over the leading role as standard bearers of antisemitism. The Russians would, however, soon make a come-back, this time with the decisive and fateful difference that they now appeared as a leading superpower in the world.

Even before the Second World War, antisemitism became a prominent ingredient in Stalin's politics. While Lenin had repudiated the antisemitism of his contra-revolutionary opponents, his paranoid successor brought it back in all its horror. As a former Orthodox Christian and even a student of theology, Stalin was certainly familiar with Christian anti-Judaism. As an atheistic Marxist, he could easily find new rationales for antisemitism.

Karl Marx

Karl Marx himself has often been depicted as a Jew by the right-wing antisemites who wanted to see the Russian revolution as part of the Jewish world conspiracy. As a matter of fact his father was a secularist, who converted to Lutheran Christianity in order to be accepted in society. Consequently Marx himself was formally raised as a Christian but probably did not get much of religious education at all and definitely not a Jewish one.

His materialistic and antireligious world-view was nevertheless imbued with antisemitism of the worst kind. Since his archenemy was capitalism, and the power of property was seen as the inherent evil of the world, the classic antisemitic theme of Jews as greedy money-lenders was not surprisingly adopted by him:

> "Let us not seek the secret of the Jew in his religion, but let us seek the secret of the religion in the real Jew. What is the profane basis of Judaism? *Practical* need, *self-interest*. What is the worldly cult of the Jew? *Huckstering*. What is his worldly god? *Money*."

With such an approach "Jew" and "capitalism" to him are almost synonymous. The Jew is viewed as an enemy of mankind. The undeniable egoism and commercialism within Christianity is then also explained as a consequence of Jewish influence. The logical solution of the Jewish problem sounds familiar to us after Auschwitz: "In the final analysis, the *emancipation* of the Jews is the emancipation of mankind from *Judaism*."[21] Even though genocide is not spelled out and probably not even conceived by the theorist Marx, there is no space for Jews in his vision.[22] Again and again history has proved that there is only a small step between the spiritual or ideological denunciation of Judaism and the Jewish people and physical persecutions. Marxism and communism are yet other examples of this.

---

21   K. Marx, *The Capacity*, quoted from Nicholls p.320.
22   The same is true for the many of the Socialist ideologists, see Nicholls p.322f.

Theory and Practice

Thus it is not surprising even Hitler expressed his admiration of Marx's anti-Jewish approach, and that Stalin reactivated classic antisemitism in the Soviet Union. He brutally purged the Communist party from Jews in the "Great Purges" towards the end of the thirties and had a large number executed or deported to Siberia. The period of 1948-1953, is sometimes called the black years, because of the Stalinist persecutions.[23] It is significant that Stalin (1879-1953) in the beginning of the fifties, at the end of his career, had a version of *The Protocols* published. Needless to say, this time they brought the message that the Jews were engineering an imperialistic world conspiracy together with the West against the Soviet Union.

Even when Stalinism was later denounced, antisemitism survived. And to be sure, virtually all the ideas of *The Protocols* were

The Jew linked to the arch-enemies in classic antisemitic fashion. The following text is attached to this cartoon from 1970: "Imperialists of U.S.A. and the Federal Republic of Germany help one of the most ruthless divisions of Zionism - Israeli rulers - to widen the aggression in the Middle East."

23   Louis Rapoport, *Stalin's War Against the Jews: The Doctors' Plot and the Soviet Solution*, Free Press, New York, 1990.

adapted to fit the communist propaganda. In numerous books and articles the power behind the various enemies of communism was ascribed to Jews. Only the terminology had changed. Who wanted to admit antisemitism after the Holocaust? So instead of "Jew" and "Jewish" the term "Zionist" was introduced with the state of Israel as the focal point of all evil (see p. 46ff,66).[24]

International Zionism was allegedly infiltrating the imperialistic and capitalist nations, forming a mighty empire of financiers and industrialists, using the mass media in their massive campaign against the socialist world, the workers and the liberation movements. The aim was the same as before: to create a Jewish world government, enslaving non-Jews. Again: Jews were the enemies not only of the Soviet people but of the whole world. It did not matter that there were hardly any Jews left in Europe after the Nazi extermination, still they were depicted as the almighty power behind opposition and insurgencies, e.g. like those in Czechoslovakia and Poland in 1968.[25]

Even more bizarre was the contention that their alleged racist ideology and superiority concept of a "chosen people" had inspired Hitler and the Nazis! Actually, Nazism, Fascism and Zionism, were labeled in the same way as equally reactionary and racist. And further back, the counter-revolutionaries, who fought against the communists during the revolution, were now depicted as Jews - i.e. a total reversal of the arguments that the Russian conservatives and anticommunists had used in those days against the Jews for being communists!

Three Features

In this vulgar propaganda we recognize some constant features of the antisemites; here I will limit myself to three:

1) To let their own opponents and hate objects be represented by a vague, secret group of conspiring Jews. In the Communist propaganda, the Zionists were consequently the embodiment of capitalism and Western corrupted values. Their atheistic propa-

---

24 See Wistrich(1979).
25 See p.12,53f,72 and further Daniel Rubin(ed.), *Anti-Semitism and Zionism: Selected Marxist Writings*, International Publishers, New York, 1987.

The Jew as the poisoner of the people is a recurrent antisemitic motif found in *The Protocols*, in the Nazi propaganda, and here in an anti-religious cartoon from 1985.

ganda was not even hesitant to present the Vatican and the World Council of Churches as their conspiring partners! One factor facilitates such accusations; the fact that Jews have been dispersed all over the world and as a result, also lived in countries and among people who were regarded as the enemy. Whoever the enemies were, Jews could be appointed as their symbol and the prime object of hatred.

2) To project their own crimes on Jews: Hitler, as well as Stalin and his successors, no doubt had ambitions of a world-dictatorship. Consequently, they ascribed such aspirations to Jews. The infiltration of the Jewish secret service was, according to Hitler and Stalin, worldwide and its methods brutal. The antisemitic projection of this was an international Jewish - now Zionist - network of spies and a plot against mankind.

In short, antisemitism is often used as a cover-up for one's own evil plans (see p.31). This pattern has repeated itself so often in history, that I would like to rephrase a well-known saying: "Tell me what they say about the Jews and I will tell you who they are!"

3) To give legitimacy to antisemitic crimes in past and present times, either by concealing, deminishing or denying them or even by contending that Jews were actually committing such crimes themselves - Jews, having been the constant victims of racism,

The Nazi poisonous mushroom from 1938 is copied by Soviet propaganda in 1973, now applied to Israel in "Arab territories."

A worse affront than linking the prime victims of the Nazis with their murderers is hardly conceivable - consequently a favorite theme in postwar antisemitism. Under the headline "Bloodbrothers," Hitler greets an Israeli soldier standing in Lebanese blood. The tree marked "Israel," is rooted in the swastika, both from 1982.

were now depicted as racists. A minority, oppressed by totalitarian and imperialist regimes, they were now portrayed as oppressors and imperialists and Israel was described as a dangerous super-power. Victims of genocide by the Nazis, they were now depicted as their collaborators and successors. The worst antisemitic caricatures of the Nazi propaganda just needed a slight retouch to serve this purpose. In the Middle East conflict, Israel has even been compared to the Nazis and accused of erecting concentration camps and committing genocide. On the denial of the Holocaust, see p.54ff.

To sum up: The myths of *The Protocols*, irrational as they are, survived and thrived in post-war communism and became a weapon in the Cold War propaganda. Their worldwide influence was considerable, since the Soviet Union exerted control not only over the numerous communist and socialist states but also over

LES PROTOCOLES DES SAGES DE SION

Die Geheimnisse der Weisen von Zion

in deutscher Sprache herausgegeben

von

Gottfried zur Beek

56

READ THE **PROTOCOLS ELDERS OF ZION** And Understand the New Deal

"...Probably the most widely distributed book in the world after the Bible..." (Norman Cohn)

Протоколы сионских мудрецов

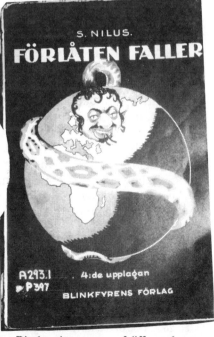

Displayed are covers of different language editions of *The Protocols of the Elders of Zion.* Top row: French, German, Portuguese, Spanish; bottom row: English, Russian, Danish, Swedish.

the Arab world and a large number of developing countries, who depended on its support.[26] A shameful monument of this antisemitic poisoning is the notorious "Zionism is racism" resolution of the United Nations in 1975. Only after the crumbling of the communist bloc could the resolution be revoked in 1991.

As a matter of fact, the post-war success of *The Protocols* in the communist world has only one parallel:

2. Islam and the Arab World

To speak about antisemitism among Arabs may seem to be a contradiction in terms. The word Semite is taken from the eldest of Noah's three sons, *Shem* (Gen 9,18). In the racial theories of the last century in Europe, Jews and Arabs together were described as a special "Semitic" race. Hebrew, Arabic and other related languages (e.g. Aramaic, Akkadian and Amharic) are therefore called "Semitic languages." In these pseudo-scientific illusions there were pure races, which could be classified according to their qualifications. Not surprisingly, the Aryan race was regarded as the superior race. Since the Jews were the most prominent "non-Aryan" people in Europe, these theories were developed in order to give scientific reasons for discriminating against them and keeping them apart from the allegedly superior race. In this frame of references the term "antisemitism" emerged. It was first expressed in 1879 as *Antisemitismus* by the German journalist Wilhelm Marr, and was then supposed to be a more respectable term than the former *Judenhass*, "hatred of Jews." It was, however, nothing but a new name for the same old phenomenon - blatant hatred of Jews, and *only* Jews; it was never used to express contempt for and to discriminate against Arabs or any other people.[27]

Therefore, the very etymology and basic meaning of the word "antisemitism" does not justify a common contention that Arabs

---

26   One of the foremost experts on antisemitism in the Soviet Union is William Korey; see e.g. his extensive study *The Soviet Cage: Anti-Semitism in Russia*, Viking Press, New York, 1973 and his article updating "The Protocols of the Elders of Zion," in *Midstream* 22,5, May, 1976, p.5-17.

27   See Nicholls p.323ff.

cannot be antisemitic, since they are Semites themselves. The contrary is true: In the post-World War II era there has not been a more fertile ground for antisemitism than the Arab (and Communist) countries. There are both religious and political reasons for this phenomenon.

Religiously, Islam has the same problem as Christianity versus the Jews: The deepest roots of their belief are found in the Bible and in Judaism, and at the same time, it claims to be the ultimate revelation of God, which has superseded and replaced the previous ones. This attitude of triumphalism can partly be regarded as Christian "export." In Islam, this ambivalence is expressed by viewing Jews and Christians both as "infidels" and as "People of the Book." Their position in a Muslim society must therefore be characterized by both subjection and protection; they are so-called "protected" people, *dhimmis*.

What this meant in reality throughout history depended on the attitude of the rulers. In the best of times (e.g. in certain areas during the Middle Ages), the situation of Jews was far better than in Christian countries. But similar to the situation in the Christian world they were constantly humiliated and discriminated against. The examples range from prohibitions of wearing dignified clothing, riding horses, building houses higher that those of Muslims, not being accepted as witnesses in Muslim courts, to even more dangerous rulings like being forced to wear distinguishing clothes such as differently colored shoes or no shoes at all, special headcovers or colored patches on their robes. This visible marking out of the Jews made them namely prone to being the target of persecutions, particularly in times of epidemics, poverty and insurgencies. The result could be forced conversions, extra heavy taxation, confiscation of property and even massacres.[28]

Just as in the Christian world, there are deep roots of anti-Jewish teaching and practice in Muslim countries. Antisemitism

28   See Bernard Lewis, *The Jews of Islam*, Princeton University Press, Princeton, 1984; Maurice M. Roumani, *The Case of the Jews from Arab Countries: A Neglected Issue*, World Organization for Jews from Arab Countries, Tel Aviv, 1983, p.23-36; Poliakov II, p.19-82; Wistrich (1991) p.195-221; Bat Ye'or, *The Dhimmi: Jews and Christians under Islam*, Associated University Presses, London, 1985.

An Arabic edition of *Mein Kampf* and a modernized book on the
medieval blood-libel from 1982, written by no less than the
Syrian Minister of Defense, Mustafa Tlas.

received new nourishment through the rapidly increasing Jewish
immigration to Palestine, mainly beginning in the second half of
the last century and culminating with the creation of the State of
Israel in 1948. The myth of the Jewish worldwide conspiracy as
spelled out in *The Protocols* and other antisemitic writings ideally
suited the Arab opposition of the Jewish immigration: Jews could
be depicted as a far more dangerous enemy than they seemed to
be. This would also make it easier to rationalize and cope with
their own political failures and defeat.

During the Second World War there were frequent contacts
between the Nazis and several Arab leaders, the most notorious
being the Grand Mufti of Jerusalem, Hadj Amin Al-Husseini,
well-known for his collaboration with Hitler and the Nazi leadership. After the war, Hitler's extermination of the Jews has often
been justified in Arab countries, and some Nazi war criminals
have found a safe haven there to continue their antisemitic activities.

Not surprisingly, *The Protocols* have been translated into Arabic and have become a bestseller in the Arab world. Antisemitic
organizations have often used Arab countries as the basis for dis-

tribution of antisemitic material. Just as in the former Soviet Union this fraudulent document has been officially sanctioned and quoted on the highest political level. Extracts and commentaries have been frequently printed in official newspapers, incorporated in school textbooks and information for the army.

In recent years the distribution is probably on the decrease, particularly in countries trying to improve the relations with the Western world. However, in circles influenced by Muslim fundamentalism, classic antisemitism continues its poisoning unimpeded. Thus, the political platform of the fundamentalist *Hamas*, "The Movement of Islamic Resistance," of 1988, borrows the ideas from *The Protocols* almost literally:

> "The Jews have taken over the world media and financial centers. By fomenting revolutions, wars and such movements as the Free Masons, Communism, Capitalism and Zionism, Rotary, Lions, B'nai B'rith etc. - they are subverting human society as a whole in order to bring about its destruction, propagate their own viciousness and corruption, and take over the world via such of their pet institutions as the League of Nations, the U.N. and the Security Council. Their schemes are detailed in the Protocols of the Elders of Zion."

The more comprehensive charter of the same movement gives further details of the alleged evil of the Jews, not even refraining from accusing them of standing behind the Second World War! The estimated support of *Hamas* in the territories occupied by Israel in 1967 amounts to approximately 40% of the Arab population. This gives an idea of the vast impact that ideas like these exert on the population up to this very day.[29]

Naturally, the commentaries of *The Protocols* in the Arab world have popularized them as to fit into the Jewish-Arab conflict. Now it is the state of Israel that is the spearhead of Jewish imperialism with worldwide ambitions. Israel is said to be only a

---

29   See Raphael Israeli, "The Charter of Allah: The Platform of the Islamic Resistance Movement (Hamas)," in: *Fundamentalist Islam and Israel; Essays in Interpretation*, Lanham, New York, London, 1993, p.123-168.

first step towards the Jewish colonization and oppression of the surrounding Arab countries.

A Coin and a Flag

Two recent examples of this modern *Protocols*-type allegations can be mentioned: The Israeli coins today usually depict motifs of ancient Jewish coins from the time before the destruction of the temple in 70 A.D. One of the first depictions of the *menorah* in the Jerusalem temple was found on such a coin. A replica now appears on the modern 10-*agorah* coin in exactly the same irregular shape as on the original. With some imagination this shape could be interpreted as a map of the Middle East, covering an area reaching at least from Egypt to Iraq and Iran. In this way the coin is used as a "proof" of Israel's imperialist ambitions - an interpretation I have heard in circles from Yasser Arafat to visiting intellectuals from Europe.

In the same line of ridiculous propaganda some students told me that their professor had "proved" the same by pointing at the two blue stripes of the Israeli flag as symbolizing the borders that Israel aims at, namely the Suez Canal or the Nile in the West and Euphrates-Tigris in the East! The truth would have been as easily accessible as with the coin: The stripes actually refer to a central Jewish religious object - the prayer shawl, *tallit*, with its classical stripes! Moreover, the flag was actually displayed for the first time in 1891, that is, even before the plans of a Jewish homeland had materialized - and even less so, any specific borders! This only shows how otherwise rational people lose their ability of even asking for the truth, when prejudice and paranoia provide the pattern of interpretation.

Antisemitism and Anti-Zionism

In the post-war survival of *The Protocols*, antisemitism has undergone a change in terminology if not in substance. Mainly two underlying factors causing this change should be mentioned. Firstly, after the destruction of European Jewry during the Second World War, antisemitism became an impossible concept because of its deadly fruits. Secondly, the creation of the state of Israel became the focus of the world in its relation to the Jewish people. In the light of this, hatred of Jews could easily be channeled into the seemingly more sophisticated and politically motivated hatred of a Jewish state.

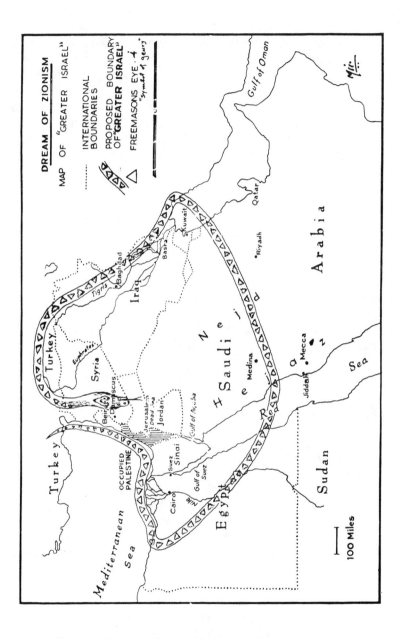

The allegedly aspired borders of imperialist Israel from the
Euphrates to the Nile in a version of *The Protocols* published
by Kuwait.

This renamed antisemitism is called *anti-Zionism,* and the anti-Zionists prefer to use the word "Zionists" rather than "Jews." In reality, however, they usually mean the same. Such an identification is in itself, however, not quite wrong, since virtually all Jews in the world are Zionists in the sense that they support the idea of national rights for the Jews in the biblical land of their fathers. The state of Israel is actually just the practical application of a dream that has lived among the Jewish people throughout the ages.

As we know, the word "Zion" is one of many names for Jerusalem, being the center of biblical Israel. Already in the Book of Daniel we learn that Jerusalem was the prayer direction of the Jews - just as the Muslims turn towards Mecca in their prayers. Every year the Passover meal has been concluded with the prayer "Next year in Jerusalem!" And for centuries the observant Jew has concluded every meal with the prayer "Have mercy, Lord our God, upon Israel Your people, upon Jerusalem Your city, upon Zion the abode of Your glory... May the Merciful One break the yoke of exile from our neck and may He lead us upright to our land." We can see how Zion / Jerusalem is the symbol of the whole land and the goal of the future dreams, which entail the end of the exile. It is just very natural, then, that the movement that emerged in the last decades of the last century, which tried to realize these age-old dreams, was called "Zionism."

It is hard to escape the conclusion that the anti-Zionists simply have found a new term, allegedly only political and thus legitimate, in a similar way as the ancient hatred of Jews was renamed "antisemitism" in the last century in an effort of making it more "scientific" and thus respectable. If antisemitism means discrimination of Jews, anti-Zionism certainly means antisemitism, when those who use it advocate a state for the Palestinians while rejecting it for the Jews. Many of those who identify with anti-Zionism are actually not discussing the borders of Israel but deny Jews the legitimate right of having a state within *any* borders. This is the context of the awkward discussion of "Israel's right to exist" - a discussion that is not applied to any other state in the world.

Such a deliberation emanates from falsifications of both Judaism and Jewish history. The Jews are then regarded as adherents of a religion only, but are not seen as a people with national rights like other nations. The fact that they have survived as a nation for more than 3,000 years is obscured or bluntly denied as is also the continued Jewish presence in Palestine throughout history. Therefore, they are depicted as newcomers and strangers in the Middle East - Western imperialist colonizers without any connection with their forefathers.

Even recent history is falsely rewritten, portraying Israel as the mighty, expansionist aggressor and the root of all evil in the Middle East. Instead of a violent conflict in which Israel was constantly attacked and acts of cruelty were committed on both sides, the anti-Zionists want to simplify reality to the relation between an evil oppressor - Israel - and innocent victims of their oppression - the Palestinians. To anyone familiar with antisemitism this echoes the tenor of *The Protocols*. It is also interesting to see how anti-Zionists on one hand see a Zionist world conspiracy - Israel and Zionism are *all over*. On the other hand Israel has no rights *anywhere*. The very name of "Israel" is then shunned like a curse and a dirty word; it should not even be mentioned among the nations. If the hot dream of antisemites is a world without *Jews*, anti-Zionists hope for a world without a *Jewish state*. The difference is more a matter of nuances than of substance (see also p.66).

Criticizing violence and injustice committed by Israel is certainly not antisemitism, as long as the same standards of criticism are equally applied to all involved in the conflict. Making Israel the root of all evil and even denying its legitimacy, however, does not escape the antisemitic label.[30] One who clearly saw the link between antisemitism and anti-Zionism clearly was Martin Luther King. When a student at a rally once attacked "Zionists," he im-

---

30   The contention that anti-Zionism is not antisemitic, since there are anti-Zionist Jews, is misleading. It is correct that there are Jews who are against the State of Israel. Their reason usually is, however, that the modern state is not religious enough - hardly the motivation of the anti-Zionists! We also have to keep in mind that even these religious Jews pray for the ingathering of the exiles to the land of Israel. Religiously they are Zionists, only the modern political realization they reject - also out of religious reasons. These orthodox Jews should therefore rather be called non-Zionists. Most orthodox Jews are, however, also political Zionists. See further Nicholls p.393ff.

mediately cut him off, saying: "When people criticize Zionists they mean Jews. You are talking antisemitism."

Just like the word "Jew" by antisemites has been linked with virtually any evil and opposite view, the same nowadays more frequently applies to "Zionist." This is particularly obvious in the Arab world, one bizarre example being the war between Iran and Iraq in the 1980's. Both are deadly enemies of Israel. Nonetheless, both sides accused one another for being part of a "Zionist" conspiracy. Along the same line, Col. Qadafi of Libya has warned of a "Zionist" plot against African countries within the realm of his political ambitions. The *Protocol*-pattern antisemitism here indeed repeats itself![31]

It can also be expected that the thin veil, which anti-Zionists have drawn over antisemitism, will fall as soon as the surroundings are ready to accept it. A recent report of a meeting of 300 Islamic students at the School of African & Oriental Studies of the University of London is alarming, even though it only deals with extremists and not with mainstream Islam: A militant fundamentalist group gave the message that the "messianic age" - the acceptance of Islam by all the earth's inhabitants - would not arrive unless there was a mass slaughter of Jews. According to the report, one public statement advocated: "We've been talking about killing Zionists. Let's not mention Zionists. The Jews are our enemy and we should finish them."[32]

To sum up: The conclusion can, without doubt, be drawn that anti-Zionism follows a pattern of falsifications and distortions of Judaism and Jewish history, which makes it not just one expression of antisemitism but its most common and typical expression in recent times.

One would like to hope that the ongoing peace process and the hoped-for results will eventually weaken this form of antisemitism. But we should not have any illusions that antisemitism as such will disappear as a result of political solutions of whatever

31 See Antony Lerman, "Fictive Anti-Zionism: Third World, Arab and Muslim Variations," in: Wistrich (1990) p.121-138.
32 Jerusalem Post, Overseas Edition, March 12, 1994, p.15.

kind. There will always be blind fanatics who are resistant to any facts, however conclusive, and to any change of their religiously or ideologically motivated hatred of Jews (see p.72f).

3. Ultra-Nationalists and Neo-Nazis

The direct inheritors of the Nazis were, for decades after the Second World War, reduced to marginal groups on the fringes of society, and were generally regarded as fanatics and lunatics. Two main factors have led to a resurgence of hatred of "strangers" and racism, in which antisemitism is a conspicuous ingredient. Firstly, the collapse of Communism has released nationalism which had been suppressed for decades. Extreme nationalism and antisemitism frequently walk hand in hand, since the Jews are regarded as international and alien. Secondly, new generations have grown up, who have little knowledge of recent history, some of whom therefore have very little sensitivity to racism and its bitter fruits. In addition, economic recession and poverty in many countries fuels extremism and the need to find a scapegoat.

Since 1990, a number of nationalistic parties have emerged in the former communist bloc, *Pamyat* (Memory) in Russia being the most well-known. A recent trial in Moscow has charged this party with having used *The Protocols* in antisemitic propaganda. The trial was constantly disturbed by members of *Pamyat* and other antisemitic groups, to whom this vicious forgery - again - is used to prove that Jews actually stood behind the communist oppression! The verdict in November 1993 pronounced *The Protocols* a forgery and sentenced *Pamyat* for antisemitic acts. To be sure, there have been several similar court cases, which all have come to the same conclusion. But this was the first such verdict in the country where the fraud originated and therefore particularly important.

Antisemites are, however, immune to facts, and antisemitism will probably continue its virulent diffusion in Russia unaffected by any court verdicts (see p.21). While this is being written, an outspoken antisemite - Vladimir Zhirinovsky, leader of a nationalistic and neo-Fascist party - has won almost a fourth of the votes for the Russian parliament. Classic themes from *The Protocols* reverberate in his speeches, as soon as he mentions Jews.

But even in other parts of Europe extreme nationalism combined with racism is a current menace. Antisemitic graffiti is frequently seen again, Jewish cemeteries are desecrated and synagogues threatened and vandalized. Nazi-inspired video games are being produced, where the players get credits for torturing and gassing prisoners and making lampshades of their skin.

The neo-Nazis and skinheads in Germany, as well as ultra-nationalist parties like The National Front in France, make headlines in the news all over the world. According to one recent report, the number of violent acts by the extreme right has increased eight times in Germany since 1990. A similar pattern can be seen in Italy, where the neo-Fascist party collected most of the votes in the last elections and got 34 seats in the Chamber of Deputies, one of which is occupied by Alessandra Mussolini, the granddaughter of the Italian dictator. A recent Prime Minister of Hungary is an admirer of the former Fascist leader, who collaborated with Hitler. Another prominent rightist politician has warned against the classic Jewish conspiracy to take over the country, and he was accompanied by racist violence all over Hungary. In Sweden, *The Protocols* have indirectly been on trial after the worst outburst of antisemitism ever. Hardly any elements of *Protocols*-inspired statements and Nazi propaganda were missing in the vicious broadcasts of Radio Islam in the 1980s. In 1989, the producer was convicted of slander and libel towards an ethnic group. Since then, the unrepentant promoters of the radio station have tried to resume their activities, hoping for protection by the "freedom of speech"-paragraph (see also p.66).

Antisemitic groups and parties emerge with a growing intensity in the U.S., Canada, and Australia. In the U.S., organizations like Aryan Nation, Ku Klux Klan and The Nation of Islam[33] are notorious. The leader of the latter organization, Louis Farrakhan, and even more respectable people, like a former aid to the mayor of Chicago, have even gone so far as to suggest that Jewish doctors invented the AIDS virus to infect black children - a modern

33 This group is not rightist and nationalistic, but when it comes to antisemitic outbursts, they differ only marginally from the first groups mentioned. Furthermore, they do not really belong under the headline of Islam, since their religious teachings are very little related to mainstream Islam.

version of the medieval Black Death-accusation and the superstition that Jews poisoned the wells and even killed Christian children! Such bizarre libels can be attributed to the idea of *The Protocols*, that Jews hate Gentiles and aim at subduing and enslaving them. To be sure, black antisemites in the U.S. have recently charged that Jews were somehow responsible for the slave trade, thus being the arch-enemy of the African Americans.[34] The fact that it is virtually impossible to find any documents that show any Jewish involvement - as contrasted to the large number of Arab slave traders - is, as usual, irrelevant to eradicate such canards. Again, it is enough to find one single Jew who was involved in that inhuman business to vilify "the Jews" (see p.28,71). No group should of course be victimized for the deeds of their forefathers. When dealing with the tragedy of slavery in the past, however, both Christians and Muslims ought to have enough skeletons to come to terms with in their own closet.

In South America, rightist antisemitism has a long tradition with the distribution of *The Protocols* and related materials continuing with little interruption even during the Second World War.

Antisemitism without Jews: Antisemitic literature has increased rapidly in Japan in recent years. The title of this book, published in 1985, is *The Secret of the Jewish Conspiracy to Take Over the World.*

34   The Nation of Islam, in 1991, published a book called *The Secret Relationship Between Blacks and Jews*, which has rightly been characterized as "one of the most sophisticated instances of hate literature yet compiled... the book massively misrepresents the historical record, largely through a process of cunning selective quotation of often reputable sources" (Prof. Henry Louis Gates, Jr., Chairman of Harvard's African American Studies Department, in an article in the *New York Times* in July, 1992).

Even in a country like Japan with almost no Jews present, *The Protocols* and a large number of similar antisemitic publications are distributed. In the most respected financial newspaper, an advertisement recently claimed that the Jews were plotting to kill half of the human race and enslave Japan! A Japanese edition of Henry Ford's *The International Jew* was recently displayed in the economics section of Tokyo's leading bookstore chain and has been promoted by a prominent newspaper as well. Many will probably believe these fantasies, and even more will think: There might be some truth behind it.

Holocaust Denial

When it comes to rightist antisemitism one feature is particularly prominent: The denial of the Holocaust. Since the perpetrators of the genocide are those with whom antisemites often identify, they have to deny their worst atrocities. That is, the purpose is to rehabilitate the Nazis and antisemitism by trying to hide the deadly fruits. They also know that the Holocaust is the main reason as to why blatant expressions of antisemitism have been outdated in the West, and by denying the Holocaust they hope to win political legitimacy.

The circle of people who deny, or at least try to minimize or trivialize the dimensions of the Nazi mass murder, is, however, far wider than the relatively limited group of outspoken neo-Nazis. Every antisemite actually has an interest in this matter, if for no other reason, just in order to remove anything that may lead to sympathy for Jews. Therefore, we find even leftist groups who want to suppress the Holocaust as unique when it comes to Jews as the prime target of undiscriminated extermination. Instead, they often stress, at the expense of Jews, the other categories of people who were exterminated - communists, Gypsies, homosexuals etc.

On a national level, several countries which were directly or indirectly involved, have an interest to suppress the Holocaust in order to escape the embarrassing and painful past.

Many Christian groups also have an interest in diminishing the evil of the Holocaust and the passivity of the churches for the same reason. To further ease their conscience, they may eagerly look for atrocities committed by Israel today, and use them - collectively and mythically, of course - to accuse the Holocaust victims of performing the same crimes as their oppressors (see p.38f).

Anti-Zionists naturally have a special reason for reinterpreting the Holocaust, and their Holocaust denial rhetoric is often masked as a critique of Zionism. The Holocaust is then portrayed as the product of yet another Jewish worldwide conspiracy to raise support for the State of Israel. In this way they follow the classic antisemitic pattern of trying to turn the crime into an accusation against its victims. Arab circles often blame the creation of Israel on the Holocaust, regarding Israel as the result of the bad conscience of the West and the Holocaust as the main factor behind the support for Israel in the world. With such a view it is natural to try to remove this cause of sympathy for the Jewish state.

General Eisenhower appears in one of the many documentary films from the liberation of the concentration camps. He says that he wants to be a first-hand witness, since the day may come when people will dispatch the Nazi atrocities as propaganda. He turned out to be a prophet. Today pseudo-historians - so-called "revisionists" - travel the world giving lectures to ardent supporters and curious listeners and publish articles, journals, and books with new "disclosures" of the "Holocaust myth."[35] In a recent statistic the number of publications promulgating such claims increased from about 100 in 1981 to 250 in 1992. It is even reported that full page advertisements on the subject have appeared in student newspapers. The tendency is obvious, and the people behind can no longer - as they would deserve - be disregarded as simply a lunatic fringe, since they are largely part of a coordinated international movement and obviously find ignorant and prejudiced target groups, who fall victim of the repeated lie.

They naturally hope that some people will regard the truth as being at least somewhere between their lies and the real truth - as if truth were a matter of opinion! But probably they will succeed, at least in part. The Holocaust is now moving from memory to

---

35   For example Robert Faurisson in France, David Irving in England, Ernst Zuendel in Canada, Arthur Butz and The Institute for Historical Review in the U.S.; see further Nicholls p.392 and Lipstadt's indispensable study.

history, which makes it more vulnerable for revisionist lies. All the eye-witnesses will soon no longer be among us. Even though the documentation is overwhelming, many people who do not remember what actually happened will not seriously study the documentation available. These are the people vulnerable to the ill-fated saying, that those who do not learn from history, are prone to repeat it - or at least to become its indifferent bystanders.

4. Certain Conservative, Liberal and Left-Wing Christians

In the aftermath of the Holocaust, large parts Western Christianity eventually began to see the connection between anti-Jewish teaching and its ultimate consequences. As we have seen, the mortal fruits of genocide had grown from a poisonous root, which had regularly been fertilized by Christian teaching of superiority and contempt. Such teaching had portrayed a more or less ugly image of Judaism as a legalistic, self-righteous religion, a cruel religion of hatred and revenge, as opposed to Christianity as the spiritual faith, the community of love. Such negative stereotypes had gradually weakened the immune defense against antisemitism in the Christian body, until there was hardly any resistance left when the Jews were indiscriminately selected for extermination.

The protests of the churches in Germany succeeded in stopping the Nazi killing of the mentally retarded and chronically ill after a toll of about 70,000; six million Jews could be murdered without any co-ordinate actions from the churches on their behalf whatsoever. Facts like these speak for themselves.

In the trials after the war, more than one Nazi war criminal tried to defend himself by referring to Christian teaching, the most notorious being Julius Streicher, the editor of the most vicious antisemitic publication, *Der Stürmer*. He could refer to Martin Luther's last book *About the Jews and their Lies*,

Luther's infamous book from 1543

which he had frequently used. That malicious book contains virtually the whole Nazi antisemitic program, short of genocide.[36] As a matter of fact there is almost nothing in the discriminatory antisemitic laws with the single exception of murder (see p.30) that had not its predecessor in previous Christian anti-Jewish laws.[37] Again, facts speak for themselves.

Reconsidering Church Teaching

Many churches were rightly in a state of shock and contrition after the war and eventually realized that there had to be a "before" and an "after" in Christian teaching and preaching, with the cataclysmic tragedy of the Holocaust as the inescapable dividing line. Only ignorant and/or insensitive Christians are blind to this reality. In 1948 the World Council of Churches assembled in Amsterdam and issued the first in a long series of statements trying to draw the consequences from the tragic past for Christian theology.

Since then, most of the larger churches have followed suit, the most important being the Second Vatican Council with the encyclica *Nostra Aetate* in 1965. Here the demonic myth that held the Jews guilty of the death of Christ was - at last - repudiated. It would, of course, have been more appropriate that we, the Christians, had seen our own needs of absolution from crimes actually

36 See Hans J. Hillerbrand, "Martin Luther and the Jews," in: James H. Charlesworth (ed.), *Jews and Christians; Exploring the Past, Present, and Future*, Crossroad, New York, 1990, p.127-150, with further references. The Lutheran churches have dealt profoundly with this dark side of the reformer in recent years. "Luther, Lutheranism and the Jews" was the theme of a conference in Stockholm in 1983 between The Lutheran World Federation and The International Jewish Committee for Inter-religious Consultations. The Lutheran delegation stated among others: "We Lutherans take our name and much of our understanding of Christianity from Martin Luther. But we cannot accept or condone the violent verbal attacks that the Reformer made against the Jews... The sins of Luther's anti-Jewish remarks, the violence of his attacks on the Jews, must be acknowledged with deep distress. And all occasions for similar sin in the present or the future must be removed from our churches." See Jean Halperin, Arne Sovik (ed.), *Luther, Lutheranism and the Jews*, The Lutheran World Federation, Geneva, 1984, p.9f.
37 Nicholls p.204ff presents an excellent comparison in parallel columns between anti-Jewish enactments in the Canonical Law of the Catholic Church and Nazi legislation.

Burning of books, regarded as heretic by the Church, was often practiced against the Jews - 15th century Italy.

committed throughout church history than giving absolution to the Jews for crimes which they had not committed! However, *Nostra Aetate* no doubt signaled a new direction of the church. Moreover, guidelines for the Christian teaching and preaching free of anti-Jewish attitudes were subsequently issued, leading to extensive studies and research on the roots of antisemitism in Christian theology. A particularly important document is the "Guidelines on Religious Relations with the Jews" from 1974, which, among others, advocates as obligatory "a better mutual understanding and renewed mutual esteem." The statement then continues to deal with the importance of a knowledge based on a living dialogue between Christians and Jews, the dangers of classic church teachings which led to contrast the Old and the New Testament and falsely depict Judaism as "a religion of only justice, fear and legalism, with no appeal to the love of God and neighbor."[38]

However, large segments of Christianity are still uninfluenced by these efforts of coming to terms with the dark chapters of church history. This is true above all for the Orthodox and Oriental churches that have many adherents in the Arab world. As a matter of fact, the harshest opposition against striking the deicide accusation against the Jews came from the Arab league governments and Arab church leaders, some of whom made direct references to *The Protocols*.[39]

Certain evangelical churches also continue the classic teaching of contempt for Jews and Judaism as if nothing had happened. And above all: It is one thing, what is stated in documents on an official level, but what is taking place at grass root level is often something quite different. What has been cultivated in almost 2,000 years can certainly not be uprooted in 50 years. Therefore,

38   See A. Roy Eckardt, *Your People, My People: The Meeting of Jews and Christians*, Quadrangle, New York, 1974, p.51; Eugene J. Fisher, A. James Rudin, Marc Tanenbaum (ed.), *Twenty Years of Jewish-Catholic Relations*, Paulist Press, New York, 1986. Collections of other Christian declarations can be found in Helga Croner, *Stepping Stones to Further Jewish-Christian Relations*, Stimulus Books, New York, 1985 (1977), and id., *More Stepping Stones to Jewish-Christian Relations: An Unabridged Collection of Christian Documents 1976-1983*, Paulist Press, New York, 1985.
39   See John Oesterreicher in: Herbert Vorgrimler (ed.), *Commentary on the Documents of Vatican II*, Herder and Herder, New York, 1969, Vol.3, p.101-116.

the spirit of *The Protocols* manifests itself within Christianity repeatedly up to this very day. Only a few examples will be given here.

So far the direct and vulgar use of *The Protocols* in Christian teaching has mostly been limited to extremely rightist and nationalistic Christian circles on one hand and to particular eschatological groups who regard the end-time as imminent on the other; sometimes they are affiliated. In the first group we find those who walk hand in hand with the political extremes, those who on their side often link their antisemitism to classic Christian teaching:

Nationalism, Christianity and Antisemitism
Supporters of the Russian *Pamyat* party are all too often seen with the cross at rallies, accusing Jews of being both communists and Christ-killers. As late as 1993, a front page article in the renowned newspaper *Pravda*, declared that Jews had murdered three Russian Orthodox monks on Easter. The article refers to Jewish sources which allegedly contain "descriptions of ritual murders of unbelievers - goyim - by Levites (with rabbinical support) and subsequent human sacrifices." The efficiency of these sacrifices - the article contends - "would be increased in proportion with the moral and spiritual level of the victim. Thus, children and clerics were preferred." Finally the editorial postscript prophesies: "In 1994 we expect to see an unprecedented wave of Judaic and Zionist propaganda."

Such an outrageous article could of course not have been published, had there not been a market among Christians for these ancient religious myths. In spite of a short apology afterwards, saying that "the article contained unjustified statements," its vicious influence cannot be overestimated and should make anyone who is concerned about the future of Russian Jewry highly alert.

An equally vulgar, yet somewhat more sophisticated, propagation of blatant antisemitism is found in a book by a certain Stan Rittenhouse in the U.S., called *For Fear of the Jews* (1982). One of the chapters in the book deals particularly with *The Protocols*, spicing them with quotations from the Bible to prove the point, like: "You are of your father the devil, and your will is to do your father's desires... He was a murderer from the beginning..." (John 8,44). Here Jews are portrayed as conspiring together with liberals and communists against Christian America as a step towards a satanic world-government. Constantly vilifying Israel, the book is able - in the name of Jesus Christ - to preclude the value of any possible good achievements of Israel as intrinsically evil: "Could it be that the Devil is attempting to imitate in this Age what Christ will do in the next?" (p.202).

Two years later another book of the same kind, yet even more vicious in its vitriolic antisemitism, appeared: *Israel: Our Duty... Our Dilemma* by a certain Theodore Winston Pike. This author tries to "explain" even the worst crimes against the Jews, like the destruction of the Temple and Jerusalem with the horrendous massacres of Jews in 70 and 135 A.D., the expulsion of the Spanish Jewry in 1492 and the persecutions of Jews in the former Soviet Union by pointing at the alleged evil of the victims. Indirectly he also condones the Holocaust by frequently applying words and terms linked with the Nazis - like genocide, Blitzkrieg etc. - on Israel. He also accuses Jews of mass murder in the past. There is no need of specifying the thoughts taken from *The Protocols*, since hardly any are missing. What is added in this disgusting book is above all a more comprehensive defamation of Judaism, built on selected and vilifying quotations out of context from the Talmud and other Jewish sources. And worst of all, the prophetic ambitions of the author remind us of Nilus: Not only is the Antichrist linked with Israel and Jews but also with the apocalyptic whore of Babylon. Significantly the chapter entitled "Death to the Harlot" does not deal with the past, but is something that this "prophet" of hatred and vile applies to present Israel!

Incredibly this book has a successor in another and more recent Christian book, claimed to be a best-seller: *Claim Your Birth-Right* by James McKeever, published in 1989. The author refers to Pike but tries maybe more than Pike to hide his deep contempt of Jews and Judaism behind the Bible. A frequent traveler to Israel he even claims to have sympathy with Jews and makes the hollow statement on the last page of the book: "Let me state one final time: we do not want anyone to become anti-Jewish or anti-Semitic. We are to love the Jews." Immediately after that statement he makes, however, very clear what is the condition of accepting them: They have to become Christians! And before the statement he has dedicated 278 pages to the most loathsome distortions and defamation of the Jewish religion that I have read in such a recent publication with Christian ambitions. Just like Pike, he uses the classic method of giving the impression of solid scholarship by quoting selectively from Jewish sources, which are chosen, just like the Nazi propaganda chose them, to prove the point that Jews are murderous, obsessed with sex - even with children - blasphemous, masters of occultism etc. And even this bigot "prophet" predicts: "Unfortunately, all that the Israelis (citizens of the State of Israel) are building today is going to be wiped out during the great tribulation..." Thus, he will see the ultimate confirmation of the poisonous statements brimming from the pages of his book.

Normally, books like these would not merit even being mentioned. I do it mainly for two reasons: These authors have an outreach beyond obscure fringe groups where anything is received and believed. Rittenhouse, a university graduate and deacon, is said to have "testified on numerous occasions before the Senate and House committees" in the U.S. Pike has also a university degree and claims to be "an evangelical writer and researcher." Dr. MacKeever, finally, "has authored eleven best-selling Christian books, seven of which have won the prestigious Angel Award." His publications have been translated worldwide. He is frequently lecturing at international conferences and claims to have shared the platform with, among others, Ronald Reagan, Gerald Ford, Alan Greenspan and "heads of governments." The power of deceit is obviously great.

The second reason for exposing these repugnant books and authors is, however, decisive for me as a Christian. What makes books like these particularly disgusting and deceptive is their pious disguise. The endless distortions of Judaism and expressions of hatred against the Jewish nation are combined with equally frequent references to the Bible and Jesus Christ. The prophetic ambitions of Rittenhouse are expressed in two quotations from the Bible, put in the beginning of the book as a prefix: 1 Corinthians 9,16 and Ezekiel 33,18-21. I can quote two other passages as a warning label on the antisemitic evil in the name of Christianity, which could actually have been used as a prefix of this booklet: "Beware of false prophets, who come to you in sheep's clothing but inwardly are ravenous wolves. You will know them by their fruits. Are grapes gathered from thorns, or figs from thistles? So, every sound tree bears good fruit, but the bad tree bears evil fruit. A sound tree cannot bear evil fruit, nor can a bad tree bear good fruit. Every tree that does not bear good fruit is cut down and thrown into the fire. Thus you will know them by their fruits"

(Matthew 7,15-20). "Take no part in the unfruitful works of darkness, but instead expose them" (Ephesians 5,11).

Christian Eschatology and Antisemitism

There is a special factor that makes this kind of religious antisemitism especially appealing to certain Christians in these days. It is probably not just by chance that so much antisemitic material was produced, disseminated and believed a hundred years ago. Throughout history, the turn of the centuries were times of vivid eschatological expectations. We are now approaching not only a new century but a new millennium. Not surprisingly, there are many groups of Christians who claim to know that the end of the present era is immanent. Therefore they also expect apocalyptic disasters to break out at any moment. Eagerly looking for a visible confirmation of their own expectations, these are precisely the kind of Christians who are vulnerable to catastrophic theories of the kind found in *The Protocols*. Again and again I have heard serious speculations regarding a Jewish Antichrist and an emerging anti-Christian world-government.

I cannot warn enough against those who are more interested in what may happen tomorrow than in what the Lord has taught us to do today. Those who take that seriously enough, will, while being aware of the signs of the times, still make the right priorities and thus be less preoccupied with end-time speculations. Be awake today, and leave it to God to fulfill his plans tomorrow: "It is not for you to know times or seasons which the Father has fixed by his own authority" (Acts 1,6). Or, as the Torah formulates the same biblical insight: "The secret things belong to the Lord our God; but the things that are revealed belong to us and to our children for ever, that we may do all the words of this law" (Deuteronomy 29,29).

Most of these groups are presumably not antisemitic; on the contrary, occasionally the same people express a deep sympathy for the Jewish people and Israel. They are simply not aware of the evil roots of some of these eschatological speculations and the danger they pose in a time of growing antisemitism. This unconsciousness makes it, however, even more necessary to expose the very nature of these allegedly biblical expectations. They have caused enough bloodshed throughout the centuries to be dispatched as just innocent faith - "expose them!"

Christian Supremacists

Even a third Christian attitude towards Jews and Judaism has to be exposed. This takes us to the opposite side of the Christian specter - liberal and left-wing groups. Usually taking the obvious evidence of *The Protocols* as a forgery seriously, they would not use them to support their anti-Jewishness. Nonetheless, they continue the legacy of the secular antisemitism that various leftist groups have cultivated for almost 200 years.

If more conservative Christians would say that a good Jew is a converted Jew, these groups would say that a good Jew is an assimilated Jew and above all an anti-Zionist or at least a non-Zionist Jew. In short, Jews should be something different than they actually are.

These are the Christians who stress the ethics of Jesus' Sermon on the Mount as the total contrast of the primitive and harsh ethics of the Old Testament and Judaism, not knowing that there is almost nothing in that sermon, which does not have its parallel in Jewish teaching. These are the Christians who ascribe almost everything that they advocate themselves to Jesus, and its opposite to Judaism: Jesus is pro-women; consequently the oppression of women emerges out of the Old Testament and Judaism. Jesus stands on the side of the oppressed as against the rich and the religious establishment; consequently Judaism represents the establishment that Jesus opposed. If Jesus is depicted as a rebellious leader of a liberation movement, Judaism is portrayed as passive and indifferent towards human misery. If Jesus is seen as a spiritual Messiah whose kingdom is not of this world, the Jewish messianic expectations are said to be earthly and political.

The contenders of such an antithetical and superior approach are often not even interested to know that there was a wide range of messianic expectations among Jews in the time of Jesus - as well as today. The point that has to be proved is made from the outset: The Old Testament and Judaism make up the dark background of the New Testament and Christianity. Do the secular and political antisemites ascribe to Jews whatever they dislike - these Christians do the same on the religious level. Curiously enough the same people are often very open to inter-religious dialogue with the non-biblical religions with a totally different openness to

Portraying the Old Testament as a Jewish book, in contrast
with the New Testament and Christianity, goes back to the
second century and continues to this very day. A typical
antisemitic illustration from Germany 1936.

facts and an attitude of listening and learning. Obviously the problem is that the inherited anti-Jewish prejudice has become so inte-
grated in their thinking, that the false stereotypes are taken as
facts which do not even need to be questioned. Many Christians,
therefore, often believe that they know living Judaism, even if
they have never seriously studied it from Jewish sources or even
talked with a Jew.

Naturally, the supremacist attitude is easily combined with a
replacement theology, according to which the new has replaced
the old, and Christianity is the new and the true Israel as contrasted to the old Israel that has forfeited its calling. Consequently,
there is no place for a Jewish people which still claims the link
with the land of their fathers. If Christ has fulfilled all the promises, there are no promises left for the Jews:

Christian Anti-Zionism

Hand in hand with the leftist and Arab anti-Zionists, these Christians therefore tend to depict Israel as a Western colonialist and imperialistic entity in the Middle East (see p.37,46ff). They blame Israel alone for the Palestinian plight but refuse to see their situation also as the result of Arab wars targeted against the very existence of the Jewish State. In the same way they blame Israel alone for the Palestinian refugee problem without acknowledging that an equal number of Jewish refugees had to leave home and property in Arab countries without any compensation. According to these Christians, Israel is the oppressor and the Palestinians the oppressed innocent victims. They therefore often add a Christian disguise to their anti-Jewishness: Jesus was always on the side of the oppressed and marginalized; consequently, Christians have to side with the Palestinians against Israel. Such a one-sided and simplified view of the Middle East conflict sometimes resembles a medieval passion play with the Palestinians playing the role of the crucified Jesus and the Israelis as the New Testament mob which screams "crucify!"

In a recent outburst of this kind of antisemitism in Sweden, a theologian - a notorious anti-Zionist who teaches on the university level - has "revealed" a conspiracy "by the Swedish Zionist lobby," engineered from Israel, against the church, the Social Democrats, the education system and freedom of speech - all this since the malicious "Radio Islam" has been exposed and sentenced for disseminating antisemitic hate propaganda in Sweden (see p.52). In the same court case a colleague of his, called as an "expert witness," defended the allegation that it is a Jewish *mitzwa* (commandment) to kill non-Jews! Moreover, he claimed such a *mitzwa* to be sanctioned and practiced in Israel today. Once again, we see an example of anti-Zionism as a transparent disguise of vulgar antisemitism in the spirit of *The Protocols*. By using anti-Israeli propaganda as a vehicle, these Christians continue the demonic picture of Jews that had disastrous consequences throughout history.[40]

---

40   See further Nicholls, chapter 11: "The Churches in the Twentieth Century," p.351-384; Norman Solomon, "The Christian Churches on Israel and the Jews," in: Wistrich, *Anti-Zionism*, p.141-154.

IV.
The Lesson

Even though the Jews are the target and the victims, antisemitism certainly is not primarily a Jewish but a Christian problem. The reason for this is manifold. Though antisemitism is neither a Christian invention, nor was genocide taught by the church, the Christian teaching of triumphalism and contempt, nevertheless provided the main fuel of antisemitism during almost 2,000 years, which paved the way to Auschwitz.

Even though most Christians could probably not foresee the horrendous consequences of anti-Jewish teaching and maybe even were convinced that their beliefs were in accord with the Bible, this does not exonerate them from responsibility. The worst crimes have been committed or condoned by people who believed that they were just. There always have been and always will be racists and oppressors who plead their cause with the Bible in their hand, fully convinced that they defend God's will. They may be exploited by callous propagandists who know that hatred is contagious and who consciously use deceit for their purpose - the history of *The Protocols* is a perfect example.

Nonetheless, everyone who consciously or unconsciously, actively or passively, has propagated antisemitic lies and contempt is a partner in crime. This is not to say that all Christians have a sort of corporate *guilt* of the kind which Christians so often laid upon the Jewish people. But it certainly means that Christians have a collective *responsibility* both to learn about and to learn from the tragic past of Jewish-Christian relations.

The first lesson, then, can be summarized precisely in this way: Antisemitism is primarily a Christian and not a Jewish problem.

This is first of all true from a Christian perspective. *The Protocols* were first published in Christian circles. And the main motifs of this forgery were rooted in Christian anti-Jewish myths that emerged in the first centuries of Christianity. We have also seen how various Christian circles all over the world up till this very day, have been instrumental in perpetuating these mythological distortions.

Further, antisemitism is not a Jewish problem when we look at it from the perspective of its victims - the Jews themselves. People sometimes ask: "How come Jews have so often been hated and persecuted?" And sometimes that question implies that there must be something with Jews that explains antisemitism, that is, something that Jews themselves actually cause. I have heard Christians contending that had Jews "only" accepted Christ or not stuck to their Jewishness, they would not have been persecuted the way they have. I have also seen articles which see the causes of antisemitic outbursts in Israeli politics in the Middle East.

Two Examples
These two examples are typical and may serve as an illustration of the deepest aspects of antisemitism. Both make efforts of accusing the victims of antisemitism as being its main cause! This would of course be a convenient way out of the inconvenient and painful process of dealing with the antisemitic evil: If only the Jews would change - one way or another - there would be no antisemitism, i.e. the antisemites and their passive bystanders do not need to repent and change! They are not even really guilty! Such efforts of victimizing the victims are therefore not surprising. No matter how preposterous they are, we have to address them.

1) The first example illustrates a common element of antisemitism: *The Jews should be something else than they are*, preferably like other people, like us! Such an attitude is, of course, not limited to Jews only, but as a minority they have always been its foremost victim.

We actually find this classic anti-Jewish model already in the Old Testament. When Haman, the arch-enemy of the Jews in the Babylonian diaspora about 2,500 years ago, presents his program for the extermination of the Jews to the king, he motivates it in the following way: "There is a certain people *scattered* abroad and *dispersed* among the peoples in all the provinces of your kingdom; their laws are *different* from those of every other people..." (Esther 3,8). They are "scattered," that is, they are a minority in the country. This is the first motivation. But that is not enough: They are also "dispersed." The Hebrew word used should rather be translated by "separated", which is then followed by the explanation that "their laws are different" - of course referring to the biblical laws. That is, they have kept their identity. They have refused to assimilate into the surrounding culture and religion. Precisely therefore Haman pleads: "Let it be decreed that they be destroyed."

A minority that keeps its identity has often been regarded as an obstacle and a threat by the powerful mainstream. There seems to be a bestial instinct in man - just as among the animals - to harass and exclude those who are different and alien. If only those odd strangers would become like all of us, then there would be no problem... Should they then, on top of all this, be a successful minority, it is even harder for the majority to bear them, particularly in times of need and distress. We live in a time of xenophobia. Our attitude to the Jewish people is a litmus test as to how we will be able to handle the dignity of any other minority group. And finally it is our own society and our own security that is endangered when antisemites and other racists vilify Jews and other minorities. Sartre's words can certainly be generalized to apply to any nation: "Not one Frenchman will be free so long as the Jews do not enjoy the fullness of their rights. Not one Frenchman will be secure so long as a single Jew - in France or *in the world at large* - can fear for his life."[41]

Haman has had followers in every generation. Along the same line, anti-Jewish *Christians* did not accept Judaism, and their solution of "the Jewish problem" was conversion to Christianity. In reality that of course meant that they should cease being Jewish.

A similar attitude characterized the enlightenment and the *liberal* movement in the 18th and 19th centuries: Jews should assimilate, again meaning that they should give up their Jewish identity.

41 Sartre p.153.

In the wake of *nationalism* in the last century, Jews were accused of being a separate nation, which was foreign and strange, having double loyalties and thus constituting a dangerous element in the nation where they lived. Many Jews tried to combat this kind of antisemitism by stressing that Jews were primarily just a religion - a "Mosaic" religion - which did not impinge on their being loyal nationalists in different countries.

When the *racist* antisemitism emerged, it stressed that Jews were a different and inferior race. Therefore it regarded assimilation as a threat and wanted to isolate them from the rest of the people. With such a view conversion did not help either. The ultimate consequence of the racist antisemitism was to get rid of the Jews - the "final solution" of the National Socialists.

Today so-called *anti-Zionists* claim to have nothing against Jews as such. But they then want to see them as only adherents of a religion, in order to sever them from being a nation and delegitimatize the state of Israel - as if it were possible to say e.g. that we have nothing against Americans but "only" want the U.S. to disappear!

The common denominator of all these attitudes is the refusal to let Jews themselves define what they are and to accept them as such. What is said in reality is this: Change or disappear - religiously, individually or nationally! For whatever reasons, to antisemites, being Jewish is always wrong. And should some Jews try to accommodate in any direction desired, in the long run it will not help, since the reason for antisemitism is to be found in the antisemite and not in the Jew.

2) The second example illustrates another common feature of antisemitism: *The double standard of judging Jews.* I call it the microscope- or magnifying glass-syndrome. Minorities have always been examined more carefully than other people. Jews have been placed under the magnifying glass. Things which could be condoned when done by other people, were exaggerated when done by Jews.

In recent years, this double standard has been more clearly seen in the Middle East conflict than anywhere else. Flaws in the Israeli democracy are magnified, while the total lack of democracy in the neighboring states is concealed. Human rights abuse by Israel sometimes make the same people utterly concerned who do not want to hear about much worse violations of human rights in other countries etc. This syndrome makes people look for a next to saintly behavior of Jews. And when they do not find what they demand, they portray what they see as a next to demonic behavior. "Jews are news" is a saying rooted in this antisemitic syndrome.

Another manifestation of the same syndrome has been aptly formulated by Anne Frank in her diary (May 22, 1944):

> "Oh, it is sad, very sad, that once more, for the umpteenth time, the old truth is confirmed: 'What one Christian does is his own responsibility, what one Jew does is thrown back at all Jews'."

The worst expression of this heinous attitude is doubtless the accusation of the Jewish people as collectively guilty of the death of Jesus. But the same pattern has constantly repeated itself. That is why *The Protocols* could be used to accuse Jews of representing the most antagonistic views. It was enough to point at one or just a few Jews as being e.g. communists or capitalists in order to victimize the whole people. One Jewish slave-trader, wealthy usurer or dishonest salesman was enough to vindicate antisemitic statements about "the Jews" (see p.28,53).

Again, antisemitism is not caused by Jews but only by antisemitic non-Jews. The alleged "causes" are nothing but triggers of a hatred that is already there. Distorting facts and making false generalizations, antisemites will always be able to find "reasons" for their contempt for Jews.

To sum up: Antisemitism is not a Jewish problem. Not because Jews are always innocent or even better than others. But precisely because they are human beings like all of us. Neither better nor worse. At the same time they are of course - like all other peoples and communities - different in certain respects. Constantly being a minority community with a strong identity, they have been scrutinized under the magnifying glass more than any other group, the purpose of which is to find "causes" for defaming and persecuting them. Antisemitism refuses to accept a simple humane approach to Jews. It is irrational hatred beyond reason.

Antisemitism Irrational

This is the main reason why it is not a Jewish problem: Antisemitism does not deal with *real Jews*, but only with vilified stereotypes. It is not based on experience, knowledge and facts, but on ignorance and prejudice, often combined with a religious and political ideology. Antisemitic prejudice turns the living, human Jew into a symbol of whatever evil is opposed, feared, and hated. It does not matter whether it is a Christian who appoints Jews as the representatives of "Law" and "deeds" as opposed to "Gospel" and "faith", or a conservative who makes them represent the dangers from the left etc.

Therefore antisemitism can flourish where there are virtually no Jews; see p.37,53f. "If the Jew did not exist, the anti-Semite would invent him."[42] I have heard the most horrendous statements about Jews from people who have never really met a single Jew. Such a lack of contact with reality actually creates the ground for antisemitic prejudice. The very absence of Jews makes it possible to believe what one wants to believe and is told to believe with no disturbing interference by reality.[43] Personal relations would make people realize that Jews are normal human beings. In times of antisemitism, Gentiles were often forbidden to socialize with Jews, from the time of the Church fathers [44] to Nazi Germany. A fraudulent lie can hardly survive if constantly confronted with living reality.

---

42 Sartre, p. 13.
43 On this problem, see Bernard Glassman, *Anti-Semitic Stereotypes without Jews: Images of Jews in England 1290-1700*, Wayne State University Press, Detroit, 1975, particularly p.190. In the time period on which the research is based, Jews were expelled from England. This case-study is typical of antisemitism in general; cf. the antisemitic outbursts in Poland and Czechoslovakia in 1968, when the number of Jews there counted in just a few thousands.
44 Thus it was decreed at the church council of Elvira in Spain about 300 A.D. among others, that Christians were not permitted to invite Jews to their homes and eat together with them.

Since prejudiced hatred is not rooted in facts but in irrational motifs - frustration and paranoia, inferiority complex and maybe even unconscious guilt - antisemitism cannot simply be uprooted through factual evidence. In this respect, Nilus was typical for the classic antisemite, when he contended that the truth is not decisive for the value of *The Protocols*; see p.18. So his kindred souls will continue to believe in them and deceive others, whatever further proofs of their fraudulent nature would be added.

Maybe it is true "that in this world we are not meant to see the truth triumph, but only to fight for it."[45] Therefore deceit has to be fought by truth and antisemitism must be countered by facts. At least in this way its malignant growth can be halted and potential victims 'immunized' against its contagious influence. We Christians have a particular responsibility, and it has never been greater than now.

A Greater Responsibility

First of all, we have a greater responsibility, because we have witnessed the bitter fruits of antisemitism more clearly than any generation before us. The Holocaust took place in our century and in the heart of the Christian world. Its documentation is beyond refutation, and in this age of mass media it is available to everyone.

Further, we have access to the tragic history of Jewish-Christian relations. Only irresponsible Christians can be ignorant of the close link between contempt for Jews in the past - e.g. in Biblical times - and contemporary Jews. Only Christians stricken by blindness, indifference, insensitivity or lack of passion for the truth, will continue to use New Testament texts as weapons against Jews, as if nothing had happened in the 2,000 years of our common history. Our generation - and all generations after Auschwitz - will face a harsher judgment for such an abuse of the Holy Scriptures than anyone before us. We will never be able to say, 'forgive us, for we did not know what we did'. Now we know. Therefore our guilt will be heavier.

45   Leslie Macfarlane in Hay p.356.

The Holocaust Lesson

A great Jewish sage of our time, Professor Emil Fackenheim, has taught what the lesson of the Holocaust should be for Jews. According to the traditional Jewish way of counting, there are 613 commandments in the Torah. Fackenheim formulates a 614th commandment, which actually expresses the lesson of Auschwitz:

> "What does the voice from Auschwitz command? Jews are forbidden to hand Hitler posthumous victories. They are commanded to survive as Jews, lest the Jewish people perish. They are commanded to remember the victims of Auschwitz lest their memory perish. They are forbidden to despair of man and his world, and to escape into either cynicism or otherworldliness, lest they cooperate in delivering the world over to the forces of Auschwitz. Finally, they are forbidden to despair of the God of Israel, lest Judaism perish."[46]

If Jews need to learn a lesson from the Holocaust, we Christians definitely have much to learn from our past. After Auschwitz Christians can no longer teach and preach about Jews and Judaism as they did before. Antisemitism is apostasy. It is blasphemous when disguised in Christian robes.

At the end of this study on antisemitism and *The Protocols*, I therefore suggest that we listen to Fackenheim and apply his teaching to ourselves. I will try to formulate a corresponding Auschwitz lesson for Christians:

> "Christians are forbidden to belittle the thoughts, words and deeds of Hitler or any antisemite before or after him, lest they become collaborators of evil. They are forbidden to keep silent, whenever contempt of Jews and Judaism in past or present times is expressed, lest they fall under the curse 'I was a stranger and you did not welcome me' (Matthew

---

46   Emil L. Fackenheim, *God's Presence in History: Jewish Affirmations and Philosophical Reflections*, New York University Press, New York, 1970, p.84. Also quoted in Nicholls p.414.

25,43). They are forbidden to forget and are commanded to admit the evil committed against Jews in the name of Christ, lest they continue 'boasting' over their elder brethren (Romans 11,18). They should study the history of the Jewish people and living Judaism, lest they continue violating the commandment 'You shall not bear false witness against your neighbor.' They are commanded to resist their urge to tell the Jews what to believe and what to do and instead be eager to listen and learn, lest they forget the words 'If you are offering your gift at the altar, and there remember that your brother has something against you, leave your gift there before the altar and go; first be reconciled to your brother, and then come and offer your gift' (Matthew 5,23f). They are finally forbidden to disqualify Judaism and despise Jewish obedience for the Torah with all its commandments, as if God had broken his covenant on Sinai and changed his eternal word, lest they lose their faith in the one God who is the same yesterday, today and in all eternity."

A serious commitment from a growing number of Christians to learn such a lesson of the past would be an appropriate way of commemorating the 90 years which have lapsed since the first publication of *The Protocols* and the 50 years after the liberation of Auschwitz and Treblinka and the other places, where the deadly fruits of antisemitism were harvested.

Only then may we hope to rejoice together with Israel, when God fulfills his promise to his people: "They that sow in tears shall reap in joy..." (Psalms 126).

BIBLIOGRAPHY AND READING SUGGESTIONS:

Arnold, Caroline; Silverstein, Herma. *Anti-Semitism. A Modern Perspective*. J. Messner, New York; 1985.

Berger, David (ed.). *History and Hate: The Dimensions of Anti-Semitism*. Jewish Publication Society, Philadelphia, New York, Jerusalem; 1986.

Bernstein, Herman. *The Truth about "The Protocols of Zion": A Complete Exposure*. Introduction by N.Cohn. Ktav Publishing House, New York; 1971 (1935).

Cohn, Norman. *Warrant for Genocide: The Myth of the Jewish World-Conspiracy and the Protocols of the Elders of Zion*. Harper & Row, New York, Evanston; 1969 (1967).

Curtis, Michael (ed.). *Antisemitism in the Contemporary World*. Westview Press, Boulder and London; 1986.

Curtiss, John S. *An Appraisal of the Protocols of Zion*. Colombia University Press, New York; 1942.

Davies, Alan T. (ed.). *Antisemitism and the Foundations of Christianity*. Paulist Press, New York, 1979.

_____ *Anti-Semitism and the Christian Mind: Crisis of Conscience after Auschwitz*. Seabury Press, New York; 1969.

_____ *Infected Christianity: A Study of Modern Racism*. McGill-Queen's University Press, Kingston, Ont.; 1988.

Dolan, Edward F. *Anti-Semitism*. F. Watts, New York, London; 1985.

Flannery, Edward H. *The Anguish of the Jews: Twenty-three Centuries of Antisemitism*. Paulist Press, New York; 1985 (1964).

Gade, Richard E. *A Historical Survey of Anti-Semitism*. Baker Book House, Grand Rapids, Michigan; 1981.

Gager, John. *The Origins of Anti-Semitism: Attitudes Toward Judaism in Pagan and Christian Antiquity*. Oxford University Press, Oxford, New York; 1983.

Gilbert, Martin. *The Holocaust: A History of the Jews of Europe during the Second World War.* Holt, Rinehart, and Winston, New York; 1985.

_____ *The Holocaust: The Jewish Trage*dy. Collins, London; 1986.

Gilman, S.L.; Katz, S.T. (ed.). *Anti-Semitism in Times of Crisis.* New York University Press, New York, London; 1991.

Grosser, Paul E.; Halperin, Edwin G. *Anti-Semitism: Causes and Effects. An Analysis and Chronology of 1900 Years of Anti-Semitic Attitudes and Practices.* Philosophical Library, New York; 1983 (1978).

Hay, Malcolm. *The Roots of Christian Anti-Semitism.* Freedom Library Press, New York, 1981 (= *Thy Brother's Blood.* New York, 1975; *Europe and the Jews.* Boston, 1960; *The Foot of Pride.* Boston; 1950).

Isaac, Jules. *The Teaching of Contempt: The Christian Roots of Anti-Semitism.* Transl. H.Weaver. Holt, Rinehart, and Winston, New York; 1964.

Katz, Jacob. *From Prejudice to Destruction: Anti-Semitism 1700-1933.* Harvard University Press, Cambridge, Massachusetts; 1980.

Klein, Charlotte. *Anti-Judaism in Christian Theology.* Transl. E.Quinn. SPCK, London; 1978.

Levy, Richard S. (ed.). *Antisemitism in the Modern World: An Anthology of Texts.* D.C.Heath, Lexington, Massachusetts, Toronto; 1991.

Lewis, Bernard. *Semites and Anti-Semites: An Inquiry into Conflict and Prejudice.* Norton, New York, London; 1986.

Lipstadt, Deborah E. *Denying the Holocaust: The Growing Assault on Truth and Memory.* Free Press, Maxwell MacMillan Int., New York, Oxford; 1993.

Littell, Franklin H. *The Crucifixion of the Jews.* Harper & Row, New York, London; 1975.

Litvinoff, Barnett. *The Burning Bush: Antisemitism and World History.* Collins, London; 1989.

Nicholls, William. *Christian Antisemitism: A History of Hate.* Jason Aronson Inc., Northvale, New Jersey, London; 1993.

Oberman, H.A. *The Roots of Anti-Semitism in the Age of Renaissance and Reformation.* Transl. J.I.Porter. Fortress Press, Philadelphia; 1984.

Parkes, James. *Antisemitism.* Quadrangle Books, Chicago; 1964.

_____ *The Conflict of the Church and the Synagogue: A Study of the Origins of Antisemitism.* Atheneum, New York; 1974.

Patterson, Charles. *Anti-Semitism: The Road to the Holocaust and Beyond.* Walker, New York; 1982.

Poliakov, Léon. *The History of Anti-Semitism.* Vol.1-4. Transl. R.Howard; N.Gerardi; M.Kochan; G.Klim. Vanguard Press, New York; 1985(1965).

Prager, Dennis; Telushkin, Joseph. *Why the Jews? The Reason for Antisemitism.* Simon & Schuster, New York; 1983.

Rausch, David A. *A Legacy of Hatred: Why Christians Must Not Forget the Holocaust.* Moody Press, Chicago; 1984.

_____ *Fundamentalist Evangelicals and Anti-Semitism.* Trinity Press International, Valley Forge, Pennsylvania; 1993.

Sartre, Jean Paul. *Anti-Semite and Jew.* Transl. G.J.Becker. Schocken Books, New York; 1960.

Segel, B. *Die Protokolle der Weisen von Zion kritisch beleuchtet.* Philo Verlag, Berlin; 1924.

Trachtenberg, Joshua. *The Devil and the Jews.* Jewish Publication Society, Philadelphia; 1983.

Williamson, Clark M. *Has God Rejected His People? Anti-Judaism in the Christian Church.* Abingdon, Nashville; 1982.

Wistrich, Robert S. *Antisemitism. The Longest Hatred.* Pantheon Books, New York; 1991.

_____ *Anti-Zionism and Antisemitism in the Contemporary World.* New York University Press, New York; 1990.

_____ *Between Redemption and Perdition: Modern Antisemitism and Jewish Identity.* Routledge, London, New York; 1990.

_____ *The Left against Zion: Communism, Israel, and the Middle East.* Vallentine, Mitchell, London; 1979.